ALIGNED
like a
LASER

Published in 2004 by Bow River Publishing
a wholly-owned subsidiary of Murphy Klatt Consulting Inc.
Calgary — Halifax — Victoria
head office:
630, 1207–11th Avenue S.W., Calgary, Alberta, Canada T3C 0M5
e-mail: mail@murphyklatt.com — website: www.murphyklatt.com
telephone: (403) 278 • 3821 — fax: (403) 278 • 1403
toll free: 1 (877) 878 • 3821

Library and Archives Canada Cataloguing in Publication

Klatt, Bruce
    Aligned like a laser : achieving organizational alignment through clear accountability for results / Bruce Klatt and Shaun Murphy — 1st ed.

Includes bibliographical references and index.
ISBN: 0 – 9730365 – 3 – 2 (pbk.)

1. Management. 2. Responsibility. I. Murphy, Shaun, 1947– II. Title.

HD58.7.K53 2004   658.4   C2004–903335–2

Editing: Bob Este and Patricia Fitgerald.
Original cover concept: *Humd!nger Communications*, Calgary, Alberta.
Cover production, interior design and project management: Jeremy Drought,
    Last Impression Publishing Service, Calgary, Alberta.
Printed and bound in Canada by *Houghton Boston*, Saskatoon, Saskatchewan

ALIGNED

Bruce Klatt & Shaun Murphy

Achieving
organizational
alignment
through
clear
accountability
for results

like a

LASER

AUTHORS OF: *Accountability: Getting a Grip on Results*

A word about our title: Aligned Like a Laser

Laser light has the following properties:

- It is monochromatic. It contains one specific wavelength of light.
- It is coherent. It is 'organized' — each photon moves in step with the others, and all photons work in unison.
- It is directional. Laser light has a very tight beam which is strong, concentrated and highly focused.

When accountability is clear and people are aligned they perform in a similar way:

- They execute based on a clear organizational strategy.
- They work together so that everyone's efforts are coordinated across the entire enterprise.
- They become a powerful and focused force.

Other Books by the Authors

Accountability: Getting a Grip on Results, (2nd rev. ed.) (2003). Calgary, AB: Bow River Publishing.

Previous editions of this best-selling book have been published by RedStone Ventures, Calgary, AB; Stoddart, Toronto, ON; and Kogan-Page, London (UK).

The Encyclopedia of Leadership: A Practical Guide to Popular Leadership Theories and Techniques (2001). New York, NY: McGraw-Hill.

The Ultimate Training Workshop Handbook: A Comprehensive Guide to Leading Successful Workshops & Training Programs (1999). New York, NY: McGraw-Hill.

Dedication

to Brian, Gary, and Gord Klatt
and Captain Walter J. Murphy

Acknowledgements

MANY OF THE PARTNERS AND CONSULTANTS IN OUR COMPANY (*Murphy Klatt Consulting*) provided essential feedback on early drafts of this book. Wes Carter reviewed original drafts and provided many constructive comments on each chapter. David Ellerington, Terry Harris, Derek Owen, Scott Richardson, and David Whitsitt also provided helpful insights and examples.

We also want to thank the following clients who have supported our work with Accountability/Alignment and generously contributed to our thinking. These include David Tuer, Doug Baldwin, Don McNeil, Jeff Buckles, Bill Sol, Dave Boone, Peter Kenyon, Jodi Drake, Jackie Chavarie, Sarah Raiss, and Tiina Moore.

Bob Este and Patricia Fitzgerald edited this book, while Jeremy Drought laid out the book and managed the production process. William Hum contributed the final cover design. All were diligent and patient, and provided suggestions that enriched the content and expression of our ideas.

Finally we want to thank our wives, Cathy Klatt and Patricia Fitzgerald, who supported our efforts and gave up family time as we struggled with countless drafts of this book over a period of nearly three years.

Contents

Introduction

OST PEOPLE IN TODAY'S WORKFORCE are experts in their own right. Whether it's mastering a complicated piece of software or managing a critical relationship, individuals have specific information, skills and knowledge that their managers — who are one step removed from the day-to-day work — often lack. As such, people must now work more independently of management, yet more interdependently with their peers.

This situation raises difficult issues of how to generate a sense of accountability and create organizational alignment among such semi-autonomous workers. The Accountability/Alignment™ process described in this book is an attempt to address these issues, and to bring current management practices in line with this evolving reality.

In the following pages we present a theory of accountability and alignment, with an emphasis on practical application.

How to use this book

1. To get an understanding of the theory and principles of Accountability/Alignment, read Part I (Chapters 1 through 5).

2. To explore the details of implementation, read Part II (Chapters 6 through 9).

3. To ensure continuing value from Accountability/Alignment, read Part III (Chapters 11 through 13).

4. To consider applications to teams, major projects, and the public service, and to reflect on the topic of accountability in everyday life, read Part IV (Chapters 14 through 17).

5. Additional examples of well written Accountability Agreements™ to supplement those in this book are available on our website at <**www.murphyklatt.com**>, as well as our our e-commerce site at <**www.accountabilityalignment.com**>.

Part I

The Operating Principles and Process

PART I WILL BE OF INTEREST TO ANYONE WANTING TO UNDERSTAND
THE BASICS OF THE ACCOUNTABILITY/ALIGNMENT™ APPROACH.

The nature of work has changed and management tools need updating.
We need practical ways to engage the commitment and productivity of
knowledge workers in the new economy. This section begins by outlining
basic beliefs about how work has changed and the implications for the
knowledge worker's business bargain. We then clarify the concepts of
accountability and alignment.[1]

Chapter 1

A New Business Bargain

ORGANIZATIONS HAVE MOVED FROM HORSEPOWER TO BRAINPOWER. Where a traditional production worker once performed a routine and closely supervised set of tasks, the knowledge worker today functions as part of a team supported by sophisticated information technology. Accordingly, the locus of control in organizations has moved from the foreman supervising the activities of subordinates, to the team leader managing the work environment and stewarding the collaborative efforts of skilled professionals.

Knowledge workers have unique information and skill that can only be put to use with their active cooperation. They are much more independent and interdependent than traditional production workers. Their expertise affords them a much greater opportunity to influence the work environment, the processes in which they operate, and the outcomes they achieve. Consequently, knowledge workers must take on proportionally greater accountability for business results. Where acknowledgement and acceptance of accountability are absent, we face increased potential for waste, confusion, corruption, poor service, high costs, and declining value.

Robert Reich, former Labor Secretary in President Clinton's administration, observes that the limited effort associated with long-term, full-time, production-based employment — which is character-ized by employees who sold their time without direct accountability

> The shift from manual workers who do as they are told, to knowledge workers who have to manage themselves, profoundly challenges social structures.
>
> Peter Drucker, Managing Oneself,
> Harvard Business Review

5

for business results — is becoming an unacceptable burden on organizations.[2] Organizations must now find new ways to engage employees and inspire determined and coordinated effort even while job security has all but vanished.

Traditional hierarchies have flattened, lessening their parental and disempowering impact on knowledge workers. Yet, some level of authority and structure remains essential. As D. Quinn Mills notes: "Perhaps someday human society will develop business organizations without any hierarchy at all, but we are not yet at that stage."[3] Organizations today must take deliberate steps to engage employees, since high levels of participation in decision making, and a sense of ownership, are central to ensuring commitment. Only where there is commitment will people do whatever it takes — within an accepted ethical and legal framework — to get results. Once committed, people will use their best judgment, take calculated risks, and find ways around barriers to success.

Some Basic Beliefs About Leading Knowledge Workers

With all that has changed in organizations, it is important to reassess the essential relationship that underpins the economic transaction called a 'job.' We begin with some basic beliefs about leading knowledge workers in organizations. These form a foundation for the operating principles of accountability and alignment that are introduced in Chapters 2 and 3.

- Everyone in business should be 'In Business'
- Busyness can consume business
- Only results count
- Enlightened self-interest motivates
- No one can do it alone
- Competing interests impair teamwork

To ensure clarity, we now 'unpack' each of these belief statements, and explore them in a little more depth.

Knowledge Work

Knowledge workers — as opposed to traditional production-based workers — conceptualize opportunities, devise solutions, and achieve business results. Their contribution comes from 'extra-role behaviors' such as innovative thinking, creativity, and teamwork. Rarely can these behaviors be specified in advance. A few examples of knowledge workers include scientists, engineers, geologists, managers, investment bankers, lawyers, consultants, systems analysts, strategists, journalists, university professors, publishers, and so on. They ask and answer questions such as: "What does it take to fully understand this situation?", "What does this situation require?" and, "Given my strengths, how can I make the greatest contribution?"

Success in Modern Organizations Requires:
- expertise and a fundamental reliance on individual intelligence, initiative, and judgment
- innovating and taking calculated risks, not just ensuring actions are defensible
- influencing and creating adult-to-adult relationships regardless of differences in organizational authority
- achieving business results, not just performing a package of tasks called a job

Accordingly, Knowledge Workers:
- want to be guided by purpose and strategy, not managed by activity
- need to know what resources and support they can expect from others
- do not assume long-term job security — everyone is now, in a fashion, 'self-employed'
- seek a reciprocal business bargain where they are recognized and rewarded for their contribution

Everyone in Business Should be 'In Business'

No employee should sit on the sidelines as an observer of the organization's business. Today, we are all the CEOs of our own area of the enterprise, and we must define our own areas of accountability. In a world where it is highly unlikely that a person will stay with one employer for a lifetime, employers become more like clients that are served sequentially, some over a period of years.

To fully participate in the enterprise, people need to stake a claim to a noticeable and significant contribution to their organization's success. They need to define their 'business within the business' in terms that are easily understood across the organization. People need to articulate their individual value proposition, and clearly state their accountability for adding value to the enterprise.

Busyness Can Consume Business

Stephen Covey's phrase, "the urgent drives out the important,"[4] has never been more appropriate since there have never been more ways of keeping busy in organizations. Communication alone can take up most of a person's available time — meetings, voice mail, email, faxes, pagers, text messaging, snail mail — all demanding our time and attention.

We are all busy and we each have only 24 hours in a day. Even worse, unproductive people keep each other busy. We need a way to focus on what makes a real difference to the organization, as well as to those who depend on our support to achieve their goals.

Only Results Count

A system of accountability is the single greatest contributor to organizational effectiveness available today. Yet effort, on its own, is not enough, and blindly pursuing activities without a sense of alignment with other peoples' expectations has become a common waste of energy in organizations. People need each other to understand their accountabilities and goals, and to be committed to their mutual success. All too often, however, some feel that it is necessary to build in

Dignity and meaning come from deep engagement.

Marvin Weisbord, *Productive Workplaces*

degrees of 'float' based on a lack of confidence in other peoples' commitment. The rationale being, if others are going to be a day late giving me what I need, I had best build in a couple of slack days just to be safe.

We once consulted to a company where an entire department went on an undeclared strike. They had made a wall chart and posted it in their meeting room. Directed at the senior executive group, the chart contained an intriguing acronym: "WYGYAT-WGOAT." Translation: "When you get your act together, we'll get our act together." This is a regrettable breakdown in accountability and mutual confidence, and occurs when busyness as a way of working is condoned.

Enlightened Self-Interest Motivates

Many of the traditional expectations surrounding employment — such as a belief that a company can provide a life-long career, or that a company is responsible for an employee's development — foster co-dependency and an inappropriate adult-child relationship. This then becomes the subtext of the employment relationship and leads to people holding dependent and unrealistic expectations such as: "If I do a good job, the company will look after me."

People need empowering frameworks in order to discuss and become clear on what they can expect from their employment in return for their contribution to business success. For many people this is a significant change in approach, and requires that they learn to be effective negotiators on their own behalf.

No One Can do it Alone

People in contemporary organizations are profoundly interdependent — no one accomplishes much without the support of others. Yet we often lionize individual contributors as if accomplishments were really theirs alone. We must recognize the complex web of collaboration that generates organizational success. We must also acknowledge the fact that people are willing to exert more of their discretionary effort if they believe that others in the organization are actively supporting and working with them.

Because they are so interdependent, individuals in modern organizations need a process to hold their manager, their direct reports, and often many others located throughout the organization accountable for supplying required resources and support. By way of example, we consulted to a multi-billion dollar off shore oil and gas exploration project on the east coast of Canada. The project manager relied on teams working concurrently in five major cities around the world. Without a solid collaborative process and the active support of these distributed teams, his role would have been impossible.

Competing Interests Impair Teamwork

One plus one is less than two ($1+1<2$) when people's interests are not aligned. As Russell Ackoff has observed, there can sometimes be more competition inside organizations than among organizations. Not only does internal competition frustrate teamwork, it often degenerates into subtle forms of rivalry based on personal rather than organizational goals.

All companies contain competing interests. These are obvious when they manifest as a battle for scarce resources or rewards, but can also show up symptomatically as performance or leadership problems that are hard to define. For example, extra staff may be required in the organization because those already present are merely keeping each other sidetracked and preoccupied by fighting over organizational turf or building internal empires.

Once people have a mutually agreeable business bargain with their employer, they have come a long way — but not all the way — to ensuring success. The complete picture requires that unclear and misaligned expectations, hidden conflicts, and overlaps and gaps in accountability are surfaced and resolved at the workgroup level. What is required is a fundamental alignment starting at the top, and cascading in an orderly and transparent fashion down through the organization. Without such alignment, resources are wasted, behavioral problems persist and accountability can never be fully realized.

We Need New Ways of Engaging Highly Skilled People

The next chapters of this book describe the tools we have developed and refined over the past decade. They form a process that generates both the spirit and the practice of individual accountability and workgroup alignment across organizations. We call the process Accountability/ Alignment. But first, we turn to the operating principles underlying this process.

Chapter 2

The Operating Principles of Accountability

THE FOLLOWING 'OPERATING PRINCIPLES OF ACCOUNTABILITY' are rooted in our basic beliefs about leading knowledge workers as outlined in Chapter 1, and have been modified only slightly from our first book (*Accountability: Getting a Grip on Results*).

Accountability:

1. is personal and not shared at the same level in an organization
2. is for business results
3. requires room for personal judgment
4. is unconditional (no excuses)
5. is primary for the organization as a whole and belongs to everyone
6. is founded on a fair business bargain

Operating Principle 1:
Accountability is Personal and Not Shared at the Same Level in an Organization

Accountability can never be shared or 'committee-ized,' and no two people at the same level of responsibility in an organization can be accountable for the same outcome. Every person's contribution is unique, and discovering this uniqueness makes it possible for each individual to identify with and take personal pride in his or her role within the organization.

> *The concept of accountability is as important as the concept of leadership.*
>
> John Gardner, *On Leadership*

Accountability can be assigned to others but it can never be abdicated. Even though a leader assigns accountability for a specific outcome to one of his or her direct reports, and does not do the work personally, the leader cannot disengage from being accountable for the final result. The selection of the individual, the clarity of the task, and the support provided to facilitate success are all part of the leader's accountability. In addition, departments, teams, committees, and workgroups of any size or description can only be held accountable through their leader, since only an individual can be accountable for the overall results of a group (we explore this in more detail in Chapter 14). Finally, accountability and empowerment must co-exist. Empowerment without accountability is chaos. Accountability without empowerment is a charade.

Operating Principle 2
Accountability is for Business Results

Accountability is about accomplishment, not busyness. Having accountability for results means that activities are not enough. Attending a meeting, giving a presentation, or developing a plan may all be useful activities, but these inputs should not be confused with business outcomes, such as signing a new contract, completing a project on time and within budget, reducing overhead costs by 10%, or cutting average customer waiting time in half.

An accountability mindset leads to an outcomes-centered versus an activity-centered approach to work. From an outcomes-centered perspective, people focus on achieving desired business results. They don't allow organizational distractions to throw them off course. They do whatever it takes within a publicly defensible framework.

Operating Principle 3
Accountability Requires Room for Personal Judgment

Accountability demands a resolute point of view. It aligns personal and organizational success and clarifies how we see the world. Having accountability for a given business result is a form of 'personal license' to exercise judgment and to exert influence. Yet, making choices leaves the chooser open to the reward and consequences of these choices. The key for management is to encourage initiative while accepting that mistakes, based on an intelligent assessment of risk, will occasionally occur.

This is why, in today's work environment, the exercise of good judgment is a core skill. Knowledge workers can be held accountable for opportunities created, as well as for opportunities missed through either commission or omission. Knowledge workers should also be well rewarded for using their best judgment, particularly where they are able to maneuver around bureaucratic speed bumps to attain successful business results.

Operating Principle 4
Accountability is Unconditional (No Excuses)

No excuse removes the fact of accountability. If you cannot deliver a business result that is within your area of accountability, then it is incumbent upon you to inform and renegotiate in a timely manner, so that others in turn can adjust and be able to follow through on their individual promises of business results.

The fact that an individual cannot deliver on a commitment is rarely the problem; instead, the issue is usually whether others have been informed of the shortfall in time to do something about it. Accountability does not imply super-human ability, although it is often surprising what people can accomplish beyond the predictable.

> The most sublime speculation of the contemplative philosopher can scarce compensate the neglect of the smallest active duty.
>
> Adam Smith, *Theory of Moral Sentiments*

Remove excuses. Especially, remove the habit of using excuses to explain failure. People and organizations are capable of meeting and even exceeding preconceived limits when a culture of accomplishment replaces a culture of excuses.

Operating Principle 5
Accountability is Primary for the Organization as a Whole and Belongs to Everyone

The most fundamental accountability is for the good of the whole, and successful organizations expect every employee to be of practical assistance in realizing the organization's goals. It means that one unit cannot succeed at the expense of the company. Neglecting this principle results in corrosive internal competition. A widespread spirit of collaboration is essential for the success of the organization. The golden eggs will be there — as long as people focus first on looking after the goose.

For example, at a large international oil and gas company, one Vice-President is accountable for exploration success in the Northern Hemisphere, and another Vice-President is accountable for exploration success in the Southern Hemisphere. Together they decide on where to explore world wide, based on what is best for the company as a whole — even though the decisions they make may result in one Vice-President being at a financial disadvantage in his own area of the business.

Operating Principle 6
Accountability is Founded on a Fair Business Bargain

Trade operates on the principle of reciprocity, and a 'fair deal' is one where each party is satisfied with the end result. Mutual satisfaction with past business transactions builds the trust and confidence to re-engage in future transactions that might involve even greater business risk. Employment is also a business transaction, albeit complex and with the reciprocity somewhat tacit. However, by failing to clearly articulate the business bargain inherent in the employment relationship, fertile ground is created for misunderstandings, disappointments, and unmet expectations.

Hesitation in making this bargain explicit is often a relic of the parent-child model of employment. Many people working inside organizations still feel that it is inappropriate or somehow disloyal to clearly state what they want in return for delivering business results. This attitude may be due to a lack of experience at making deals, a lack of confidence in stating what one's services are worth in the marketplace, or perhaps some reluctance to acknowledge that, fundamentally, employment is a business bargain, and that skills are 'for sale.' Regardless of the reasons for reticence, there can be no genuine accountability without articulation, negotiation, and agreement on the positive consequences that an individual can expect to receive for successfully delivering promised business results.

It's Not as Simple as a Carrot and a Stick

We're not suggesting that the simple promise of an extrinsic reward such as a salary increase or an annual performance bonus is all there is to constructing a 'fair deal' in the workplace. Pure behaviorism — the carrot or the stick — is far too simplistic. Many factors play into motivation at work: an individual's nature, the work itself, the work environment, working relationships, and so on.

People are not that easy to understand, let alone to motivate. An individual's motivations are often complex, variable, and rarely fully understood by him or her self. In addition, few of us are free of conflicting motivations. As much as money is a motivator for many people, prestige or recognition may be seen as more valuable to others. For example, we know of one client who valued his title of Vice-President more than the role of 'manager' at another organization, even though the latter position came with a much higher salary despite the less prestigious title. On the other hand, another client of ours has continuously sought assignments regardless of title or salary considerations. Her focus has been on developing her expertise, a broad network of colleagues, and a comprehensive understanding of the many divisions in her company. Her actions are based on long-term career aspirations more than on immediate title or compensation considerations.

Focus on both Long- and Short-term Positive Consequences

Short-term positive consequences have to do with annual salary, bonuses, and assignments, whereas the long-term positive consequences could encompass the whole arc of career success, and might include overall credibility, professional respect, and even the notion of leaving a legacy within a department or organization. The balancing of short and long-term positive consequences can be delicate. At times, an individual may need to forgo a short-term gain for a job well done, and focus more on a long-term positive consequence, such as working toward a promised promotion a year or two into the future.

The most unfortunate and ill thought-out cases occur when consequences are arbitrarily assigned by the employer, without any acknowledgement of the underlying business bargain that forms the very basis of the employment relationship. Ironically, in these situations, the best of intentions can push employees to disengage or leave an organization, because they receive rewards they do not value or that have no logical connection to their accountabilities — a scientist, for example, being given a corner office on an executive floor when she spends all her time in the lab, or being given a impressive job title even though she has very little concern for titles. Perhaps what the scientist really wants is a new piece of lab equipment, or the freedom to do an unconventional piece of research. Finding out what motivates each individual, and building this into an explicit business bargain, is fundamental to constructing a set of positive consequences that people will value and work hard to achieve.

Building an explicit business bargain requires constructive discussions of positive consequences between the employee and his or her employer. This requires that both parties have some skill in negotiating and communicating. Accordingly, both employees and employers need to help each other learn while they practice this essential aspect of their business relationship.

Examples of Positive Consequences

Positive consequences which energize people might require a direct investment of money, or they might require no direct cost at all. In addition, they might be personal, or they might be a request for departmental resources or support. The range is potentially infinite. Here are just a few examples.

Examples of Long-term Positive Consequences:

- Consideration for promotion within next 2 years
- Be offered a supervisory role by Q4 next year
- Personal satisfaction that employee pride in the Company has been restored
- Investment community and shareholders find the Company an attractive opportunity for the future
- Customers regard us as a desirable organization to do business with over the long term
- A larger role in future investor meetings and events representing the Company
- The opportunity to act in a senior operating role in an extended absence situation
- Continued and increased role beyond current department
- Acknowledgement by one's peers for an outstanding contribution to the organization or one's profession

Examples of Short-term Positive Consequences:

- Six week vacation next fiscal year
- Choice in selecting assigned company vehicle next year
- Nomination for a professional award
- Opportunity to participate in the Corporate Executive Development Program next year
- Opportunity to participate in the development of a flex work program
- Renewal of contract for another three years
- New uniforms for Security Department team
- Two visits to field operations by my manager during the next fiscal year
- Bonuses for myself and all sales team members

Making Accountability Real

This chapter has outlined the nuggets that we have mined through many years of experience, and from hundreds of conversations and consultations. We hope that these six operating principles of accountability will serve as pointers for you, so that accountability becomes real in your organization.

Chapter 3

The Operating Principles of Alignment

WORKGROUP ALIGNMENT IS PARTICULARLY IMPORTANT in knowledge-based roles where people work interdependently and inevitably depend on the efforts and support of others in order to be successful. It builds community, without which a workgroup has little hope of engaging people's commitment, energy, and focus. We define alignment as the application of individual accountability at the group level. It starts with clear individual accountability for contributing to the organization's success, and exists when all gaps and overlaps have been resolved and the level of mutual support has been agreed upon.

The alignment process legitimizes raising difficult conversations, creates a positive context for resolving disagreements, and fosters an environment of mutual support. The following operating principles guide the alignment process.

Alignment:

1. links individual accountabilities at the group level
2. resolves gaps and overlaps of accountabilities and goals
3. achieves agreement on mutual support
4. requires a foundation of strategy, structure, and leadership
5. is best achieved using the 80/20 rule
6. is dynamic and requires regular tune-ups

The following expands on these principles:

Operating Principle 1
Alignment Links Individual Accountabilities at the Group Level

Alignment is the process that brings accountable individuals together into an effective whole, whether in a workgroup, a team, or an entire organization. Alignment is first attained at the workgroup level, and then across interdependent workgroups.

Having each member of a workgroup complete his or her Accountability Agreement, and then ensuring that all group members understand and support the business bargain that is articulated in each agreement, goes a long way toward achieving alignment. For example, a CEO of a pharmaceutical firm was unhappy with his Research Director's performance. Clinical trials were running behind schedule. The Research Director had not fully accepted that clinical trials were part of her accountability — until the facilitated conversation took place, and agreement on the ownership of clinical trials was reached during the alignment meeting.

We have seen numerous examples of well-intentioned individuals caught in dysfunctional workgroups, where mutual blaming and skillful non-cooperation became the norm. Mistrust and withheld support is even more common between workgroups. Organizations rarely have effective processes for identifying and resolving these instances of subterranean acidity. As a result, a collective history of hard feelings can accumulate where people have been 'pretending not to notice,' even though the presence of resentment is palpable.

What is remarkable about these situations is how easily long-standing disputes can be resolved when individuals participate in a positive and structured discussion, with a clear understanding of their own business bargains in hand. In this way, the alignment process resolves misalignments among individuals, strengthens mutual understanding and support, and most important of all, improves individual and workgroup productivity.

Some Symptoms of Misalignment

- People find it difficult to coordinate their work and develop a spirit of cooperation.
- There are orphan projects or tasks where no one takes accountability.
- People seek authority for decisions that they could or should be making themselves.
- People are working hard yet results are not being achieved.
- There are a lot of zombie problems — killed many times, yet they rise again.
- People or workgroups are unknowingly working on the same task.
- Managers are doing or re-doing (or checking and re-checking) the work of the people who report to them.
- Direct reports are not clear on their leader's accountabilities or goals.
- Tasks are performed but not to the standard, or in the way that is required by customers.
- There is frustrating and unproductive internal competition in the organization.
- People resist joining the workgroup or becoming a member of the project.

Operating Principle 2
Alignment Resolves Gaps and Overlaps of Accountabilities and Goals

We define a *gap* as an accountability for a business result that no one seems to own, while an *overlap* is an accountability for a business result that two or more people claim to own. Alignment requires articulation and resolution of gaps and overlaps of accountabilities within workgroups, and among interdependent individuals across the entire organization.

During the alignment meeting, members of the workgroup review each individual's Accountability Agreement to negotiate and validate the individual's perspective on their role. Gaps and overlaps of accountability are surfaced and resolved during this process.

Gray areas are identified where accountabilities have been poorly defined, even though they may not necessarily be in dispute. Tensions, which have been downplayed or considered undiscussable in the organization, are raised constructively and resolved. Such conflicts usually result from gaps, overlaps, and misunderstandings of individual accountabilities, which, when not discussed and resolved, result in faulty expectations, internal competition and blame.

Operating Principle 3
Alignment Achieves Agreement on Mutual Support

An *interdependency* exists where, in order to deliver on his or her own accountabilities, an individual relies on another person to deliver a given product or service. Alignment involves acknowledgement of inter-dependencies and documenting explicit agreements for mutual support.

By way of example, a number of Executive Assistants, each working solely for a different executive in a company, operated largely in isolation from each other and had never been particularly close as peers. With a little encouragement, they decided to align their Accountability Agreements. They quickly found value in cooperating and sharing ideas. Now they regularly help each other with peak workloads. They also meet monthly as a group to support and to learn from each other.

It is not unusual for tensions and conflicts between workgroups to be built into the organization design. As such, some tensions might not be resolvable at the level at which they were created. For example, Sales could be put into conflict with Production when orders are placed which are impossible to deliver on time. Alignment between such workgroups sometimes draws attention to basic and often long-standing problems in an organization that might not otherwise get addressed.

Systemic conflict requires a 'referee', often a manager with overall decision-making power to ensure that agreements are made in the best interests of the organization. In addition, aggregate requests for support may exceed available resources (e.g., demands on a leader's time, budget allocations etc.). This needs to be identified and resolved at a senior level to avoid constant and intractable conflict at lower levels in the organization.

Collaboration, Not Isolation

Some managers have asked us if Accountability Agreements could be used as a 'set of blinders' much like people once used MBO (Management by Objectives). Recall that one of the knocks against MBO was that people would ignore important tasks or refuse to help a colleague, saying something like: "Sorry, that's not in my list of goals this year." This was very much an extension of the old job description mentality where steep hierarchies created silos that allowed and even encouraged people to claim a set of tasks, and then to act as if what really mattered was keeping others off their turf. This kind of thinking is no longer sustainable since business processes today cross many organizational boundaries, and marketplace survival demands that everyone emphasize the interests of the organization as a whole.

The interdependence of all the members of an orchestra may be a useful analogy for demonstrating how Accountability/Alignment leads to embracing and not excluding productive options. Knowing your role as a violinist keeps you out of the percussion group, but demands harmony with all of the other players, as well as concern with and sensitivity to the overall performance of the orchestra as a whole. Success requires individual accountability — the best performance possible — as well as alignment across the entire orchestra.

Operating Principle 4
Alignment Requires a Foundation of Strategy, Structure, and Leadership

Individual accountability within a workgroup, team, or organization cannot be aligned without a sound context of credible strategy, workable structure, and effective leadership.

Organization Strategy

The company or workgroup strategy needs to provide hope for a prosperous future, which can be realized through people's harmonized efforts. Parallel to our fifth operating principle of accountability that states: 'Accountability for the organization as a whole belongs to everyone,' alignment is only possible where key corporate goals are understood and supported across the enterprise or business unit. People need to understand the strategic goals of the organization, how they will be achieved, and how difficult strategic tradeoffs will be resolved.

While competitive circumstances can make it difficult to communicate all aspects of corporate strategy, there is always a core set of goals that everyone in the organization should understand. To build and grow alignment, however, organizations need to do more than simply inform employees of core goals. They need to actively involve employees in dialogue about the importance and interdependence of key corporate goals. Only in this way will employees develop the perspective and depth of understanding they require for aligning their individual contribution with organizational strategy.

Organization Structure

Once strategy is set, organizational structure then needs to be determined prior to implementing any organizational improvement initiative. While some structures will work better than others in a given set of circumstances, the literature on organizational design suggests that the idea of 'one right structure' is a fallacy, and that under the right circumstances almost any structure can be made to work. It is therefore important to not be forever distracted by questions of organization structure. Rather, it is better to agree on a structure, implement it, and get on with the business tasks at hand, while accepting that the structure will never be exactly 'right,' and as such, may be continually refined and improved.

Accountable Leadership

No business process can make up for a lack of leadership. Enlightened leaders are essential to creating a work environment where the full benefits of the Accountability/Alignment process can be realized. The credibility of leaders will be assessed by how they first hold themselves, and then others, accountable. Where leaders lack courage or are disinterested or unresponsive, they have little to offer others by way of direction and inspiration.

Operating Principle 5
Alignment is Best Achieved Using the 80/20 Rule

At a certain point, workgroups start to experience diminishing returns from any additional time spent in alignment conversations. Organizational effectiveness, like personal physical fitness, reaches

> *There is always an optimal value beyond which anything is toxic.*
>
> Gregory Bateson, *Steps to an Ecology of Mind*

an optimum level for the purpose intended. This is why we suggest evoking the 80/20 rule (the Pareto principle) in the alignment process. This principle says that 20% of misalignments likely cause 80% of the problems or difficulties in workgroups and organizations. Beyond this 20%, continuing the alignment process is likely to yield diminishing returns.

Operating Principle 6
Alignment is Dynamic and Requires Regular Tune-Ups

The status quo cannot be maintained in today's rapidly changing and highly competitive business environment. The fact is that you can't stay fit, organizationally or personally, by resting on your laurels. Alignment requires regular tune-ups to remain relevant and useful. As with Accountability Agreements, maintenance is essential — that is, an ongoing and regularly scheduled process to ensure that newly emerging misalignments are sought out, brought into the open, discussed, and resolved.

Alignment Lays the Groundwork for Success

The result of a successful alignment process is that workgroup members:

- understand the specific results that each group member is promising to deliver

- are clear on working relationships and interdependencies within the group
- hold themselves individually accountable for clearly defined business results
- are able to depend on specified support from other group members
- agree on the leadership style and work culture that the group wants to sustain, and
- agree on how they will use Accountability/Alignment on an ongoing basis to achieve business results

Such behavior and attitudes form a foundation for a continuously improving team, and an engaging work culture.

Now that we have discussed the basic operating principles of accountability and alignment, Chapter 4 provides an overview of the process itself. Later chapters focus on 'how it's done' — how accountability and alignment are implemented, operated, and sustained so that promises can be made and kept.

Chapter 4

The Accountability/Alignment Process

THE CONCEPTS OF ACCOUNTABILITY AND ALIGNMENT can't be left in the abstract. Based on the principles articulated in Chapters 2 and 3, the Accountability/Alignment process described in this chapter provides the necessary structure for bringing these concepts to life. It creates an environment in which people can perform at their best. It starts with development of individual Accountability Agreements, moves to aligning these within workgroups and then across interdependent workgroups, and finally focuses on exercising the discipline to ensure desired results are achieved.

The Accountability/Alignment process has three steps:

Step 1: Accountability
- develop individual Accountability Agreements

Step 2: Alignment
- align (realign) Accountability Agreements

Step 3: Achievement
- use the process regularly to ensure business results

These steps shape the essential foundation for the practice of accountability and workforce alignment in organizations. To ensure that accountability can become a reality, we now explain each of these steps in detail.

Step 1: Accountability

Accountability is articulated through the creation of a document called an Accountability Agreement. This creates a context for success by outlining the individual's business bargain and making his or her contribution visible within their organization. It is a brief — 2 to 3 page — overview of the business outcomes an individual is promising to deliver, and outlines the resources and support that he or she needs from others in order to deliver these results.

The process for developing an Accountability Agreement and an outline of the components of an Accountability Agreement, are provided in the sidebars that follow. Chapter 6 provides guidelines for writing an Accountability Agreement as well as several examples of well written Accountability Agreements.

Process for Developing an Accountability Agreement

Prepare
Read this book in preparation for writing your Accountability Agreement.

Draft
Write your Accountability Agreement with the help of a skilled consultant.

Upgrade
Get feedback on your Accountability Agreement from your supervisor, co-workers, or others, and revise your Accountability Agreement accordingly.

Negotiate
Negotiate and agree on support required from others, and on positive consequences with your supervisor.

Sustain
Use your Accountability Agreement and update it as necessary to ensure it remains current and valuable.

Components of an Accountability Agreement

The following 7 elements describe the individual's business bargain within the organization.

Business Focus Statement

The business focus statement describes your business within the business. It is your value proposition within the organization, the umbrella under which all your accountabilities are organized.

Operational Accountabilities

Operational accountabilities are brief, clear statements of the business results you are promising to deliver. They describe what gets accomplished.

Leadership Accountabilities

Leadership accountabilities are also expressed in terms of outcomes, and describe the work environment you will create to make exceptional performance possible. They concern how work gets accomplished.

Support Requirements

Success in organizations today demands a significant level of teamwork and reciprocity. Support requirements, expressed in terms of specific behaviors, describe the resources and contributions that you need from others in order to achieve your accountabilities and goals.

Goals

Operational and leadership accountabilities set the context for goal setting. Goals are measurable or observable results that you are promising to accomplish within a given time period. The accomplishment of goals contributes to achievement of your accountabilities.

Sustainment Plan

The sustainment plan describes how you will keep your Accountability Agreement up-to-date and focused on business results as circumstances change.

> ### *Positive Consequences*
> Positive consequences are confidential between you and your immediate supervisor. They describe your part of the business bargain with your company — the rewards you will receive in return for delivering on your accountabilities and goals.

Step 2: Alignment

The alignment meeting is a constructive business dialogue, focused on getting things done. When all members of a workgroup have completed their individual Accountability Agreements, the workgroup is then ready to hold their alignment meeting. This involves dialogue and negotiation, and ends in clear understanding and agreement on each group member's Accountability Agreement. These agreements are then upgraded and revised based on alignment discussions.

More specifically, alignment involves identifying and resolving gaps and overlaps of accountabilities within a workgroup, identifying key work interdependencies, and then ensuring that people have the resources and critical support they need to achieve their accountabilities and goals.

The alignment process makes difficult issues discussable. No one individual has to raise what might be a controversial and perhaps threatening issue on their own. Rather, the process ensures that misalignments are put on the agenda through the identification of gaps and overlaps in individual accountabilities and goals.

Once expanded to other workgroups, the alignment process ensures that every member of the organization is clear on his or her accountabilities, and that each element of every Accountability Agreement is understood and agreed upon. This focuses energy and eliminates distractions across the entire organization. It also provides a renewed sense of confidence since people publicly declare their promises of support and business results.

Accountability Agreements need to be updated and realigned within workgroups on a regular basis as circumstances change or memories of agreements fade.

The Alignment Process

Prepare

Circulate the complete package of workgroup Accountability Agreements to all group members prior to the alignment meeting.

Align

- Conduct the workgroup alignment meeting. Resolve gaps and overlaps of accountabilities. Agree on interdependencies and mutual support requirements.
- Revise Accountability Agreements based on decisions at the alignment meeting.
- Where necessary, align Accountability Agreements with key individuals in other workgroups.

Realign

- Realign Accountability Agreements as circumstances change to ensure they are kept current, relevant, and valuable.

Step 3: Achievement

Individuals experience immediate value in this process after completing their Accountability Agreement. Organizations experience value through the alignment process. However, lasting achievement is only realized through maintaining the discipline. In their insightful book, *Execution: The Discipline of Getting Things Done*, Bossidy, Charan and Burck note that: "Putting an execution environment in place is hard, but losing it is easy."[5] It takes discipline to break old habits and maintain new ones such as regularly holding people accountable for delivering promised business results. Accountability/Alignment provides a reference point and reminder for helping leaders to 'follow through,' and ensure that the agreed business results are realized.

Keep Accountability Agreements Visible to Maintain Momentum

One way of keeping Accountability Agreements visible is by posting progress measures where organization members can read them and provide comment. On one project we worked on, everyone seemed to appreciate the immediacy of having this information posted outside each person's door.

We like the metaphor of a dashboard where only the few critical measures are kept prominent and in plain view. This purpose is served by Accountability Agreements which are kept current and aligned, and used regularly to monitor execution within the workgroup.

Put Accountability Agreements on the 'Intranet'

Several organizations have developed intranet support for communicating Accountability Agreements internally. The network of accountabilities represents the 'org chart' of the future, illuminates what have previously been invisible yet critical relationships, and outlines how work is actually accomplished — as opposed to mapping administrative hierarchies and building impenetrable silos.

Model Accountability

Leaders play an important role in keeping Accountability/Alignment visible. They need to share their Accountability Agreements widely, and have their direct reports refer to Accountability Agreements when alignment issues surface. Employees quickly follow the model, and start using the language of accountability in their everyday work. As one CEO client of ours stated: "Accountability/Alignment left a cultural legacy. It was much more than just a new process."

Synchronize the Process with Related Processes in the Organization

Accountability/Alignment needs to be linked with related processes including goal setting, performance management, recruiting, coaching, and even new employee orientation practices in order to avoid confusion and duplication. As with other managing systems, it is a matter of a) deciding how processes will mesh, b) eliminating duplication of effort, and c) ensuring that people in the organization understand how processes work together.

Using Accountability Agreements to Ensure Business Results
Accountability/Alignment conversations are best conducted in workgroups, as opposed to one-on-one meetings with the boss. The process is one of dialogue, learning, and support, not judging and blaming. As progress is discussed on all aspects of accountability each group member comes to know where every other group member is succeeding, where each is struggling, and where each requires additional resources and support. In some organizations, this will represent significant culture change as well as ongoing skill development.

Accountability, Alignment, Achievement — Three Steps to An Accountable Organization

It is always a bit of a gamble to try to improve an organization. The key to success is a simple and consistent approach, coupled with an emphasis on perseverance until the new way of working has had time to prove its value. Yet, the rewards from successful organizational effectiveness initiatives can be remarkably large relative to the investment. Once these rewards become visible senior leaders eagerly do whatever is necessary to sustain the new way of working.

Chapter 5

The Old Tools Have Lost Their Luster

Accountability/Alignment is sometimes perceived, at first glance, to be another HR (Human Resources) process. However, a closer look and some first hand experience reveals fundamental differences that deliver business value.

HR tools such as performance appraisal and MBO (management by objectives) represented real progress in their day. Their most enlightened features allowed people to participate in setting goals, and to receive annual feedback on their performance. The implementation of these tools was in part based on the recognition that people could influence their own work without having to be continually directed by supervisors. Nevertheless, most of these HR tools have their roots firmly planted in the industrial age and the old production model of management, and require updating if they are to be of value in today's 'post industrial' and knowledge-based organizations.

The following widely used HR practices are all under some pressure to adapt in order to remain relevant in the contemporary work environment.

- Job Descriptions
- Behavioral Competencies
- Management By Objectives (MBO)
- Performance Appraisal
- Performance Contracting / Service Level Agreements
- Performance Management
- RASCI Charting

The familiarity of these traditional approaches, combined with some similarities to Accountability/Alignment, can lead to a degree of confusion in principle and application. The following discussion is intended to dispel any misunderstandings.

Job Descriptions

Job descriptions list such things as job title, salary range, tasks to be performed, education requirements, special conditions of employment, and the level of supervision received and exercised. When kept up-to-date, they provide a foundation for determining job level and pay grade (defensible compensation), and guide hiring and employment equity practices. Yet, the individual's unique and dynamic business bargain is not addressed in a job description, and the notion of having the person 'force fitted' to the job is exceedingly out of date.

Behavioral Competencies

Behavioral competencies are the skills, knowledge, and behaviors that are considered significant to individual performance and career development. Examples include technical competence, leadership ability, teamwork, communications skills, change management skills, cultural sensitivity, and so on. The notion that success in organizations is derived from a list of desired behaviors is obviously an oversimplification, but it does have some particular uses. The ability to describe a job abstractly, such as a response to the question: "What skills are required of a project engineer?" helps in job evaluation and recruiting.

However, behavioral competencies cannot describe the particular job perspective that a talented jobholder will adopt, the complex constellation of experiences and skills that the jobholder will apply, the results the individual is expected to deliver, or the support he or she will be able to rely on from others. To be successful, each knowledge worker must shape the job to suit his or her own unique combination of expertise, perception, and interests.

Management By Objectives (MBO)

MBO has been in and out of fashion since the 1960s. It is an ongoing effort to facilitate recording and achieving goals (the terms 'goal' and 'objective' are usually seen as synonymous). The major disadvantage of MBO is that in some organizations it has become something of an elaborate game. Managers push for lofty goals in the hope that something more modest will in fact be achieved. This results, over time, in a sort of 'goal inflation' where people request a two-month delivery time for a two-week goal, knowing that the boss will likely set the target at one month. MBO can also lead to an overemphasis on goals that are easily measured versus goals that are more qualitative in nature, leading to an excessive focus on the short-term.

MBO is a useful but limited tool in that it lacks the context of a complete business bargain. Accountability/Alignment provides the essential context in knowledge-based work environments where commitment and interdependence are critical to success.

Performance Appraisal

A performance appraisal serves as the basis for administering an organization's compensation and formal discipline programs. It guides decisions ranging from determining pay raises to promoting and firing employees. It involves observing and evaluating an individual's job-relevant strengths and weaknesses, and provides a 'seemingly rational' and 'legally defensible' basis for people decisions. Performance appraisal programs also request that at least a minimum level of performance feedback be provided to employees.

Performance improvement in knowledge-based work environments is best supported with multiple stakeholder input — feedback involving the individual, the workgroup, the immediate supervisor, and internal customers. This needs to be done in a supportive and challenging work environment, where accountabilities are clear, effort is aligned, and agreed upon resources and support are provided.

Performance Contracting / Service Level Agreements

Performance contracting — often known as Service Level Agreements (SLAs) — involves agreeing on a contract for a specified piece of work, and using the contract as a basis for program review and assessment. It sets out performance standards which guide the service provider, and outlines criteria for performance monitoring and evaluation.

In some ways, SLAs are like insurance policies. They don't guarantee service, but they do provide a framework for monitoring as well as upfront agreement on reparation, should things go wrong. Compared with Accountability/Alignment, SLAs tend to be quasi-legal, rather than aspirational in nature. Like MBO, they emphasize the short-term and largely ignore strategic, contextual, and, most significantly, the issues of interdependence and collaboration.

Performance Management

Performance management combines performance appraisal with the upfront involvement of employees in planning their work and setting goals. Performance management plans are beneficial when discussed regularly between an individual and his or her immediate supervisor. In practice, however, these plans have tended to be used sporadically — often only annually — and so are frequently outdated by the time they are next used for discussion purposes.

Further, when accompanied by rating or ranking (usually for the purpose of serving the compensation system), performance management can also encourage competition rather than cooperation within workgroups, thereby impeding the development of effective teamwork. Finally, performance management is often distorted by the powerful and all-too-human effect of attribution theory. This theory states that where we relate well with someone, we are more likely to evaluate his or her performance positively. However, if someone rubs us the wrong way, we are more inclined to evaluate his or her performance harshly (see sidebar).

An Example of Attribution Theory at Work

I Like Him   *I Dislike Him*

He Succeeds

- he's smart and deserving
- he has earned his success
- he's dedicated and works hard
- only he could have pulled this off

- he's just lucky
- he was at the right place, at the right time
- anyone could have done what he did
- we all contributed; he just got the credit

He Fails

- he faced impossible circumstances (e.g., inadequate resources)
- nobody could have done the job
- in view of the difficult situation, it's amazing that he did as well as he did

- there is an inherent flaw in his character
- it was just a matter of time before his attitude and habits caught up with him
- he's not real bright
- only he could have made such a mess

Attribution theory (see sidebar) is very much 'in play' in modern organizations because of the complex and dynamic nature of knowledge-based work. While the underpinnings of attribution theory will always be present to some degree when knowledge workers' contributions are evaluated, a lot can be done to alleviate this problem such as the provision of a clear strategic business bargain, aligned and made public across the organization. This creates a solid and defensible foundation upon which to base an evaluation of individual contribution.

RASCI Charting

RASCI is a task execution tool. It helps organize an array of activities into a coordinated effort. By listing who will do what, when, and with what support, a RASCI chart indicates the permission, progress, and support conversations that need to occur to accomplish a goal.

RASCI is an acronym for:

- **R**esponsible (Who is responsible for this task or activity?)
- **A**pproval/**A**uthority (Who makes the final decision?)
- **S**upport/**S**takeholder (Whose support is needed?)
- **C**onsult (Who needs to be consulted for their input?)
- **I**nform (Who needs to be kept informed?)

The weakness of RASCI is that it does not address the managerial and relational context so essential in modern organizations. The contribution of knowledge workers (e.g., intelligent risk-taking, building coalitions) is not a simple 'to do' list of tasks. Success is based on commitment to clear outcomes and alignment of specific support requirements. Within

A Partial Example of a RASCI Chart

Example: Pat has the goal: 'All users of the new CAD system will be able to perform to standard as defined in the CAD manual, by December.' A partial example of a RASCI chart might look something like this:

Actions Required	By when	Pat	Joe	Tom	Training Vendor	Steering Committee	Others
Identify all users needing training	June 3	R			S	I	C – HR
Identify general training objectives	June 5		A	R	S		
Set up training schedules	November 1				S	I	C – Corp. Services

the context of clearly aligned accountabilities, however, RASCI is useful for graphically coordinating actions required to accomplish a set of goals.

Moving Past the Limitations of Traditional HR Approaches

The traditional HR approaches need to evolve to fit the modern workplace. Where this evolution is not occurring, such approaches will continue to be viewed with cynicism by operating departments, and seen as necessary yet irritating anachronisms. Organizations need to ensure that their HR processes are consistent and integrated with knowledge-based work environments. Our answer is Accountability/Alignment. It provides the missing link in organizational effectiveness that is urgently needed. It does this by documenting the unique and strategic contribution of individual knowledge workers, each of whom must balance an entrepreneurial passion for his or her own role while embracing a sense of accountability for the organization as a whole.

Part II
Implementing and Getting Value from the Process

PART II WILL BE OF VALUE TO THOSE CONSIDERING IMPLEMENTATION OF ACCOUNTABILITY/ALIGNMENT.™

If you want to first consider ways to assess the value of this approach, then go directly to **Part III: Sustaining the Process**. If you want to learn more about how it has been applied on teams, on projects, or in the public sector, see **Part IV: Specific Applications**.

The following chapters describe implementation and application of the Accountability/Alignment™ process. They provide guidance on writing individual Accountability Agreements® and aligning these within workgroups and across organizations. Strategies for getting started and managing implementation are examined. The final chapter in this section focuses on 'capturing the value' and guides ongoing use of Accountability/Alignment™ in daily work.

Chapter 6

Writing an Accountability Agreement

PEOPLE RARELY APPRECIATE THE CONCEPT OF ACCOUNTABILITY until they have engaged in the personal struggle to think strategically about their role — and to put it in writing. With a little coaching people can articulate a more influential perspective and distinct contribution for themselves within the organization.

Writing a compelling Accountability Agreement is an acquired skill. The examples provided below will guide you through the process. However, we encourage you to use the assistance of a trained consultant the first time you write your Accountability Agreement. The differences in impact and overall effectiveness are substantial.

Writing an Accountability Agreement is a Reframing Experience

People act on what they believe, so if you're going to help them change, you have to help them change their frame of reference so they can see things differently. Working from an energizing 'frame of reference' will result in a significant and meaningful Accountability Agreement. As a concrete example, a Manager of Regional Exploration in one of our client organizations was promoted to Vice-President of World Wide Exploration. Initially, his thinking about his new accountabilities was too narrow and more along regional lines. His accountability was reframed from 'replacing depleting reserves' to 'growing reserves to enhance medium and long-term company growth'. This reframing moved him from

---

Articulating Accountability at the Right Level: Examples of Frame Sizes

The 'frame size' or perspective that an individual takes toward his or her role can vary considerably. The right frame is one that challenges the individual to expand his or her influence, but also one in which business results can be significantly influenced.

Lower: Working within approved budgets
Higher: The financial health of the organization

Lower: Setting annual operating targets
Higher: Annual and long-term operational targets articulated and met

Lower: Employees understanding the company's obligation in times of lay-off
Higher: Employees understanding all aspects of their employment relationship

---

thinking essentially in terms of tactics about maintaining the status quo, to thinking more strategically about growing the company.

Challenge the Status Quo

We encourage an optimistic perspective when writing an Accountability Agreement. Optimism and a level of confidence in the future are required for any meaningful accomplishment, and the acquisition of any significant new skill takes time. Organizational improvement requires enough optimism to believe that a better future is possible, and enough experience to know that getting there is never quick or easy.

When writing your Accountability Agreement we challenge you to articulate what your role *should be*, not necessarily what it is today. For example, a client was in the role of 'Acting Manager.' Her initial thinking was to write her Accountability Agreement describing her old role, since she had not yet been offered the manager's role on a permanent basis.

She was encouraged to be more assertive and to write her Accountability Agreement describing the full impact she felt capable of making. She wrote a powerful agreement and began to fulfill this role almost immediately. It was hardly a surprise that she was formally promoted to the manager's position a short time later.

Well Written Accountability Agreements

A well written Accountability Agreement demonstrates the courage to be answerable for your part of a business. It outlines the specific, significant, and unique contribution of the individual, and the negotiated relationship that he or she has with others in the organization. It empowers the individual to use influence to achieve business results. It is also brief (just 2 or 3 pages) and serves as a valuable communications tool within the organization. (Three examples of well written Accountability Agreements are provided at the end of this chapter, while further examples can be found on our website, **www.murphyklatt.com**).

Developing the Accountability Agreement

The following components are discussed in the order that they are typically addressed when developing an Accountability Agreement.

- Parts List
- Business Focus Statement
- Operational Accountabilities
- Leadership Accountabilities
- Support Requirements
- Goals
- Sustainment Plan
- Positive Consequences

Examining each of these components, and reflecting on well written examples of each, will aid the writing of a concise and powerful Accountability Agreement.

Parts List

The parts list helps you to prepare to write your Accountability Agreement. It is a brainstormed list of what you do, or should be doing (e.g., tasks, activities, projects, things that take time at work). There is no need to put this in any particular order. Its only purpose is to serve as a reference as you write your Accountability Agreement.

Business Focus Statement

This is your value proposition within the organization. It describes your 'business within the business,' and is the umbrella statement that covers all facets of the role that is uniquely yours. A well written business focus statement should express a level of aspiration and emphasize what your role should be, not just what your role is today.

Example of a Well Written Business Focus Statement
(taken from a CEO's Accountability Agreement)

- Restore HiTech to strong financial health and position the Company for long-term growth and shareholder value

Operational Accountabilities

Operational accountabilities must challenge you to exert your influence within the organization. Write these in terms of the outcomes that will be achieved through your best efforts. In some cases, you might also state the impact that achieving a given business outcome will have on organizational success. Be as specific as possible. Avoid generalizations, challenge the current concept of your role, and articulate your role as you want it to be, not necessarily as it is at the present time.

Examples of Well Written Operational Accountabilities
(taken from an Administrative Assistant's Accountability Agreement)

I am personally accountable for:
- The Vice-President's calendar reflecting her priorities
- A smooth running office (e.g., fielding and referring inquiries, troubleshooting office and computer equipment problems)

Operational accountabilities can usually be expressed in 8 to 15 statements when they are clear and concise. The description of inputs like 'understanding the client's needs' or 'developing the project plan' is unnecessary — such inputs are assumed. Talking about an outcome that is well beyond the individual's influence, such as 'the client's annual gross revenue,' is unrealistic. Focusing each statement at the right level of outcome — an outcome that the individual can significantly influence — is the key to writing operational accountabilities well.

Leadership Accountabilities

Management of the work climate is an essential part of the leader's role. In a positive work climate with constructive social norms, even the most reluctant employees feel compelled to cooperate. For this reason, leadership accountabilities need to focus on the 'people side' of your role. They describe how you want to work with others in the organization (e.g., direct reports, peers), what you seek to contribute as a leader, and the type of work environment you want people to co-create.

Your values as a leader should be clearly visible in your leadership accountabilities. They set the tone for leadership style, and introduce the notion that 'it starts with me.' While some leadership accountabilities may be 'held in common' with others in your organization, you are nonetheless personally accountable for delivering on your own leadership accountabilities. These can usually be expressed in 3 or 4 concise statements.

Examples of Well Written Leadership Accountabilities
(taken from an HR Director's Accountability Agreement)

I am personally accountable for:
- The success and development of my direct reports
- An HR department that models the desired culture for the organization as a whole

Support Requirements

Support requirements outline how others — including the person that you report directly to — are accountable to support you. They list the resources and support you require from others so that you are able to deliver on your promises of business results. You would normally write support requirements for your boss, direct reports, peers in your workgroup, and a few specific internal clients. As with other sections of your Accountability Agreement, your support requirements need to be discussed, negotiated, and agreed upon as part of the alignment process.

Examples of Well Written Support Requirements
(taken from an Information Technology Director's Accountability Agreement)

I require the following support from:

SENIOR VP MARKETING AND IT
- Involve me early in discussions that impact IT resources and its customers
- Continue to support negotiated priorities

EXECUTIVE VP EXPLORATION, COO, AND CFO
- Understand interdependencies between your part of the business and IT
- Support me in my role of balancing department priorities with IT resources

Specific support requirements are much more powerful than general requests. In this way, there is single point accountability for providing support.

Goals

Goals are milestones for assessing progress toward fulfilling your accountabilities. They need to be measurable or observable, time based, and realistic. It's that simple. Keep goals brief, challenging, and attainable. Although goals need to focus on achieving operational accountabilities, we recommend having at least one goal based on your leadership accountabilities and one based on your professional development, during each operating period.

Example of a Well Written Goal
(taken from an Accounting Manager's Accountability Agreement)

- Internal management report for 'incentive compensation calculation' signed off by Corporate Committee by February 28th.

Sustainment Plan

Sustainment involves reviewing progress on individual accountabilities and goals, and updating and realigning Accountability Agreements as required.

Example of a Well Written Sustainment Plan
(taken from a Production Engineering Coordinator's Accountability Agreement)

- Review progress towards goals with Engineering Coordinators' Team monthly

The action required by this sustainment plan is clear and unambiguous. Others can comment on its execution or omission.

Positive Consequences

Positive consequences are the rewards you will receive for fulfilling your accountabilities and goals. Your job is a business bargain. Your knowledge, skill, experience, and commitment are your capital. Positive consequences represent a fair return for using this capital well.

Articulate positive consequences that are significant and realistic given the circumstances of the organization. Don't bet against yourself with bravado statements such as: 'Fire me if I don't succeed!' Just ask for what you can reasonably expect in return for delivering on your promises. It is very important to remember that this is the only section of your Accountability Agreement that is not discussed at the alignment meeting. Positive consequences are confidential between you and your supervisor.

Examples of Well Written Positive Consequences
(taken from a Business Support Team Leader's Accountability Agreement)

- Opportunity to participate in the flex work program
- Top quartile treatment re: incentive program

The Accountability Agreement is Only the First Step

The key to writing a valuable Accountability Agreement is keeping it simple, and at the right level of outcome, so people across the organization are able to understand the promises you are making.

The Accountability Agreement is only a record of the challenging and revealing thought processes that produced it. As such, it provides a physical vehicle for sharing insights, and makes it possible for people to reflect and comment on each other's roles and promises of business results. But the document itself won't create accountability. Accountability exists in the domain of action, and requires commitment and follow-through. The Accountability Agreement provides the map. Accountability is the journey.

Examples of Well Written Accountability Agreements

The following examples of Accountability Agreements are from different industries, disciplines, and levels of seniority. Although identifying details have been removed, these still reflect the unique operating environment, leadership styles, wording preferences, and desired emphasis of the individuals who created them with our consulting assistance.

Accountability Agreement
Brian Sullivan, CEO

Business Focus Statement

Restore HiTech to strong financial health, and position the Company for long-term growth and shareholder value.

Operational Accountabilities

I am personally accountable for:

a) A corporate strategy that restores credibility in the future of the Company

b) An organization that is aligned and moving in a clear direction

c) Board support for the management team and corporate direction

d) HiTech viewed as a strong and contributing corporate citizen

e) HiTech recognized as a leader in fibreoptics

f) Employee pride and investor confidence in HiTech

Leadership Accountabilities

I am personally accountable for:

a) Success of my direct reports through dialogue and coaching

b) Company-wide focus on profitability, cost awareness, and business competitiveness

c) High-performance culture achieving aggressive business results

Support Requirements

I require the following support from:

Executive Team

a) Members articulate and meet their own accountabilities and goals

b) Members work well as a team and focus on the success of the company as a whole

Employees

a) Employees actively support the direction of HiTech

b) Deliver on your promises

c) Invite your best and brightest colleagues to apply for work at HiTech

Goals

a) Reduce general and administrative expenses by 20% this fiscal year

b) Prioritize and reduce capital expenditures by 20% this fiscal year

c) Increase fibreoptics market share by 5% by December 31

d) Procurement Process Improvement business benefits realized in this fiscal year

e) Accountability Agreements and alignment completed for executive by September 30

f) ROE of 12%

g) Customer retention rate of 92%

h) Top 3 concerns from Employee Survey resolved and communicated throughout the organization by June 30

Sustainment Plan

a) Review results quarterly with executive team (execution review meeting)

Positive Consequences

a) Personal satisfaction that the company is meeting customer and shareholder expectations

b) Personal satisfaction that employee pride in the Company has been restored

c) Investment community and shareholders find the Company an attractive opportunity for the future

d) Customers regard us as a desirable organization to do business with

e) Board follow through on my overall compensation package

Accountability Agreement
Jane Alberti, Production Engineering Coordinator

Business Focus Statement

Optimization of the field production system to achieve budget and production targets.

Operational Accountabilities

I am personally accountable for:

a) Production engineering projects that result in stable production

b) Service rig programs and projects that stimulate increased production

c) Environmentally safe operation

d) Cost effective engineering solutions

e) All regulatory requirements met

f) Technical integrity of all production engineering projects

g) A community of practice for production engineering that shares knowledge across all field operations

h) Communication between Engineering and Operations personnel to enhance planning, coordination, and implementation of projects across the operational area

Leadership Accountabilities

I am personally accountable for:

a) Competent production engineering staff

b) An entrepreneurial and high performance work environment

Support Requirements

I require the following support from:

Engineering Manager

a) One-hour meeting every two weeks to review projects and update issues

b) Continue providing me with decision-making latitude for my areas of accountability

c) Work with me to resolve difficult HR issues

d) Provide the resources I need to get the job done (people equipment, facilities, budget)

Human Resources Coordinator

a) Ensure consistency of HR practices across all field locations

b) Continue university recruitment to ensure I have the summer students and new graduates required

Engineering Coordinator

a) Keep me informed of operation and engineering issues that impact the Business Unit

b) Work collaboratively to ensure the best engineering solutions are achieved

c) Keep informed of new technology that could enhance production

Field Foreman

a) Keep me informed of operation issues that impact the Business Unit

b) Keep me informed of new processes and technology

c) Identify the 'highest production potential' engineering projects, and get actively involved in helping me create solutions

d) Supervise service rig programs and projects to ensure objectives are met

Direct Reports

a) Compliance with all health, safety, and environmental regulations

b) Achieve one or two development goals this year

c) Involve the field foreman and operators in the development of solutions, so they have the background they need to support the solution in the field

Service Rig Superintendent

a) Keep me informed of operating costs and failure frequency issues

b) Comply with all health, safety, and environmental regulations

c) Develop programs that minimize service rig downtime

Goals

a) Zero safety or environmental incidents

b) Keep operating costs below targets set by management

c) Complete staff plan and restructuring of field assignments by December 31

d) Complete my Accountability Agreement and review with direct reports, peers, and Manager by February 1
e) Develop and implement a template for service rig program by June 31
f) Develop and implement a cost-tracking system by March 31
g) Develop and implement a well-failure frequency system by August 31
h) First meeting of 'community of practice production engineers' by October 15
i) Complete TCE course by December 31

Sustainment Plan

a) Review progress towards goals with Engineering Coordinators monthly
b) Review current and projected 'progress satisfaction' with direct reports every 4 months

Positive Consequences

a) Leather jackets for my team if we meet our targets
b) Company sponsored family day

Accountability Agreement
Syd Smith, VP Human Resources

Business Focus Statement
HR systems and an organizational culture that ensures our people are fully engaged in the Company's success

Operational Accountabilities
I am personally accountable for:

a) An organization that values diversity, learning, and wellness

b) Accurate, accessible, and secure Human Resources information

c) HR systems and practices that attract, develop, and retain talented people

d) People being compensated accurately and on time

e) People understanding all aspects of their employment relationship

f) Leadership capability and succession readiness within the company

g) The orientation and transition of employees

h) Executive Team support of HR's strategy, systems, and practices

i) Compliance with all HR related regulations and legislative requirements

j) HR Strategy being reflected in the Company's strategic plan

k) Employees understanding their accountability and being aligned to support each other's best efforts

Leadership Accountabilities
I am personally accountable for:

a) An HR department that models the desired culture

b) The success of my direct reports

Support Requirements
To succeed I require the following support from:

SVP – HR & Corporate Services

a) Provide immediate feedback and ongoing coaching on my leadership and the achievement (or lack of achievement) of my accountabilities

b) Provide the resources HR requires to be successful

c) Be the advocate for staff and HR issues at the executive table

Executive Team Members

a) Help me initiate and integrate HR initiatives that address business concerns

My Direct Reports

a) Articulate and meet your accountabilities and maintain your alignment

b) Model effective leadership (e.g., leverage our diversity, work collaboratively)

c) Ensure consistency of HR practices across the organization

d) Work together as a team and support each other

My Administrative Assistant

a) Understand my business and priorities, and manage my time accordingly

Goals

a) Accountability/Alignment process complete across top 5 management levels by Q4

b) Accountability/Alignment integrated with performance management and staffing systems by Q2

c) Communications strategy developed and approved by Q3

d) Community investment / contributions policy approved by June 15

e) Internal web pages redesigned by the end of September

f) PM and accountability feedback completed for all employees by Q4

g) M&A transition sessions rolled out to all employees in Q2

Sustainment Plan

a) Semi annual meetings with each of the Executive Team members

b) Quarterly reviews with SVP - HR & Corporate Services and with my direct reports

Positive Consequences

a) Financial reward arrangements as negotiated

b) Continued and increased role beyond HR

c) Larger role in investor meetings and events representing the Company

d) The opportunity to act in a senior role during an extended absence

Chapter 7

Getting Your Workgroup Aligned

THIS CHAPTER DESCRIBES HOW TO SUCCESSFULLY DESIGN and conduct the alignment process. This process integrates Accountability Agreements to ensure:

- all accountabilities and goals that need to be articulated within a given workgroup, department, or organization are owned (no gaps)
- every accountability and goal has only a single owner at any given level in the organization (no overlaps)
- interdependencies are recognized so that mutually supportive bargains are agreed (as articulated in the support requirements section of each individual's Accountability Agreement)

The alignment process recognizes that many things can fall into a 'no man's land' in organizations. Orphan projects or organizational goals may be important, yet neglected for any number of reasons (e.g., a history of failure, insufficient support). In alignment discussions, any lack of progress is flagged for discussion, and systemic issues driving success or failure are addressed. Such conversations have immediate benefit for workgroup morale, as members become increasingly confident in their ability to tackle and resolve issues that may have been ignored because they were seen as too threatening, too complex, or impossible to resolve.

Once a workgroup is satisfied with its own internal alignment, individuals then align with key interdependent individuals in other workgroups, such as service suppliers or internal customers. Since organizational processes often cross department boundaries, aligning across workgroups creates synergy throughout the entire organization. This enhances the ability to correct misunderstandings, eliminate roadblocks, and generate innovative solutions to problems that cross organizational boundaries.

Alignment Within Your Workgroup

The preceding chapter provided guidance on writing an Accountability Agreement. Once each individual's Accountability Agreement is in good draft form you are ready to optimize your whole group's performance through the alignment process. As a specific form of change initiative, alignment requires skilled consulting support. A consultant who is experienced with group and organizational dynamics, teambuilding, leadership development, and role negotiation may have the right background. The following steps highlight the alignment process.

Ensure Accountability Agreements are Ready for the Alignment Process

Trying to align without well written Accountability Agreements is frustrating and chaotic, as people are not able to talk about their roles, goals, and support requirements in concrete terms. As a result, groups miss opportunities to deal with complexity and differences, and may fail to recognize and resolve work and role misalignments.

Once all group members are satisfied that their individual Accountability Agreements describe their unique and complete business bargain, you are ready to begin the alignment process. It takes two drafts to get an individual's Accountability Agreement just right. This usually involves running the first draft past a few co-workers for feedback and then revising it based on this feedback. The time spent preparing Accountability Agreements pays off in productive dialogue, and especially in the efficient use of workgroup time during the alignment meeting.

Prepare for the Alignment Process

Anticipate potential or key misalignments that need to be resolved, and summarize these on one page using each group member's

Accountability Agreement as the reference. Next, think through and articulate the specific outcomes you want to achieve from your workgroup's alignment meeting. Finally, prepare and circulate an agenda to group members in advance of the meeting.

In an organization where we were recently consulting, a number of potentially derailing issues were identified as we prepared for the alignment meeting. The group's leader was advised of these issues in advance, and so was not caught off-guard when they emerged during the meeting. This proved to be an important factor in proactively resolving a number of difficult and potentially embarrassing misalignments within the workgroup.

Complete the Alignment Process at the Workgroup Level

While having a schedule, structure, and specific outcomes is important, the alignment process is rarely routine or completely predictable. As with any group learning process, it tends to be organic and evolve in ways that the group can integrate given their work culture, relationship patterns, and the competence of their leader.

Leaders often prefer to have a consultant facilitate the alignment meeting. In this way, the leader can focus on the task at hand, instead of on group dynamics and the meeting process. It also gives the leader the opportunity to fully engage in the dialogue and participate as a 'first among equals' within his or her workgroup. This can be a strong team bonding experience.

One manager in an oil and gas exploration company poked and probed and asked great questions during the alignment meeting. His questions helped ferret out clear accountabilities and alignment about whether the engineering manager or the field operations manager was accountable for 'down-hole' costs (a drilling term). These costs were skyrocketing, and bringing them under control required establishing and assigning clear individual accountability. Once this level of clarity was achieved costs began to decline almost immediately.

After the alignment meeting, each group member will need to revise his or her Accountability Agreement. These are then circulated within the workgroup and elsewhere in the organization, as required. As stated earlier, a common practice is to place Accountability Agreements on the organization's intranet. In this way, they are accessible on demand across the organization.

Aligning Accountability Among Interdependent Individuals in Different Workgroups

Once alignment is completed within a workgroup, individuals can then take the opportunity to align their Accountability Agreements with a small number of key people in other workgroups — people with whom the individual is interdependent, or from whom specific resources and support are required. This also creates an opening to discuss vital issues with suppliers and customers, be they internal or external.

The key difference in aligning the Accountability Agreements of individuals in different workgroups — versus within a single workgroup — is that higher-level managers might be needed to act as 'tie breakers' in cases where agreement is not forthcoming. Within workgroups, the group leader plays this role. Across workgroups, however, it is sometimes necessary to appeal to a higher court (i.e., a senior manager) to resolve gaps or overlaps of accountability. This may help to ensure that each individual's articulated support requirements are reasonable, given the right priority, and resourced appropriately.

The Facilitated One-on-One Alignment Meeting

We advise working particularly difficult and time-consuming alignment issues 'offline,' prior to or following the workgroup's alignment meeting. In particular, a facilitated one-on-one alignment meeting between two individuals whose work is interdependent can be useful where difficult or deeply entrenched misunderstandings, misalignments, and relationship issues exist. This allows two people to resolve conflicts, build working relationships, clarify performance expectations, and ensure clarity on the support they require — all without using valuable workgroup time in the process.

Agenda for a One-on-One Alignment Meeting

- review and clarify expected outcomes for the meeting
- allow 1 hour to review each individual's Accountability Agreement
- record issues, gaps, and overlaps as the meeting progresses and resolve these immediately, where this is possible
- summarize agreements reached
- summarize remaining gaps and overlaps
- agree on action plans and next steps
- debrief the meeting

The Greatest Leverage is in Alignment

While an Accountability Agreement helps an individual to think strategically about his or her role, the greatest organizational benefit comes through the alignment process. Aligning Accountability Agreements in workgroups, and then among interdependent individuals in different workgroups, removes barriers and concentrates the organization's energy on strategic objectives. To this end, the prerequisites for successful alignment are thorough preparation and skilled consulting support. This ensures a constructive context, allowing workgroups to identify and resolve difficult issues while strengthening working relationships and commitment to business results.

Alignment Meeting Materials

The following reference materials guide planning and facilitation of the alignment meeting.

1. Suggestions on the Alignment Meeting Agenda

Meeting Purpose

- Align members of the workgroup to ensure clear expectations, strong mutual support, and a follow up strategy for delivering promised business results.

Meeting Outcomes

- Gray areas' are clarified and misalignments resolved (i.e., gaps, overlaps). Where this is not possible during the meeting, agree on how misalignments will be resolved at a later date.
- Interdependencies are identified and support requirements are agreed.
- Support requirements with people outside the workgroup are identified, and a plan agreed to secure this support.
- Leadership accountabilities are aligned within the group. Agreement on the type of work environment and leadership style that is important to the group's success.
- Agreement on how the group's set of Accountability Agreements will be communicated within the organization.
- Agreement on a sustainment plan to ensure Accountability/Alignment remains up-to-date and valuable to the workgroup.
- Agreement on actions that will be taken following this alignment meeting.

Alignment Meeting Pre-Work

- All group members review each other's Accountability Agreements, note areas requiring clarification or discussion, and come prepared to discuss these at the alignment meeting.

Consultant Pre-Work

- If an 'alignment discussion guide' is to be used, prepare these materials in advance of the alignment meeting. (The alignment discussion guide is reviewed in the last section of this sidebar.)
- Summarize a preliminary list of gaps and overlaps, and discuss with group leader prior to the alignment meeting. (This list usually evolves from discussions while facilitating completion of each individual's Accountability Agreement.)
- Agree on key outcomes the leader requires from the alignment meeting.

Options for the Alignment Meeting Agenda

Introduce and set the context for meeting:

- review and agree on the outcomes being sought from the meeting.
- agree on the meeting agenda.
- agree on meeting process and groundrules.
- review a preliminary list of gaps and overlaps (this list is prepared prior to the meeting) and ensure agreement on the most important misalignments to resolve.

Three process options:

- **option 1**: work from the preliminary list of gaps and overlaps, and tackle each misalignment, one at a time.
- **option 2**: use an 'alignment discussion guide' to work through each element of group members' Accountability Agreements.
- **option 3**: begin with the group leader and review each group member's Accountability Agreement in turn.

As the meeting proceeds:

- ensure understanding of each group member's business focus statement, accountabilities, support requirements and goals.
- identify misalignments (gaps and overlaps), and, where possible, resolve these during the meeting.
- identify interdependencies and agree on support requirements across the workgroup.

Ending the meeting:
- agree on a follow up plan to ensure this work is sustained and promised results are delivered.
- summarize agreements (e.g., gray areas clarified, gaps and overlaps resolved, interdependencies identified).
- review other action steps agreed to at this meeting, and when these need to be completed.
- debrief and evaluate the meeting.

Some Suggested Meeting Groundrules
- All team members participate in the meeting.
- Come prepared with a good second draft of your own Accountability Agreement.
- Be open to constructive feedback and to negotiating changes to your Accountability Agreement.
- Keep track of changes to your own Accountability Agreement as the alignment meeting progresses.
- Make clear requests and suggestions for changes to other people's Accountability Agreements.
- Commit to following-up on action plans that are agreed to at the meeting.

2. A Checklist for the Workgroup Leader

Preparing for the Alignment Meeting
- Contract a consultant who is experienced with this process. Getting the right help can make the difference between surfacing and resolving tough issues, versus just superficially addressing misalignments.
- Be clear on the key areas of misalignment that you want to resolve at the alignment meeting.
- Defuse predictable, dysfunctional conflict prior to the meeting. Have any necessary conversations in advance, where these are critical to ensuring successful alignment and mutual support at the meeting.
- Book at least a half-day when all group members can attend.
- Distribute the alignment meeting agenda prior to the meeting.

- Distribute copies of each individual's Accountability Agreement with the agenda.
- Advise group members of pre-work requirements (e.g., prepare questions regarding each other's Accountability Agreement).
- Discuss any special roles you want people to play at the meeting.
- Prepare your opening remarks.
- Arrange administrative requirements (e.g., room setup, refreshments, lunch).
- Assign the accountability for revising each individual's Accountability Agreement as a result of agreements reached at the meeting — this ensures revisions get completed.

Starting the Alignment Meeting

- Welcome people and orient the group to the task at hand (e.g., explain what you want to get out of the meeting, clarify ground rules, review roles).
- Set the context and climate for the meeting. Aim for a meeting environment of mutual problem solving (e.g., supportive, open dialogue; mutual discovery).

Advancing the Alignment Meeting

- As the meeting progresses, summarize and record resolutions of gaps and overlaps, agreements on mutual support, and action plans.
- Keep the meeting focused. Remind people of outcomes and time constraints.
- Distinguish between unanimity (we all agree) and consensus (most agree and others can at least 'accept' the decision).
- Use a 'common text' to record decisions and action plans (e.g., a whiteboard).
- Maintain a balance between staying on time and providing the group with time for meaningful dialogue on their accountabilities, goals, and support requirements.

Ending the Alignment Meeting

- Review progress, next steps, and action plans.
- If needed, set a date and agree on the next alignment meeting agenda.
- Evaluate the meeting. Ask: "What went well?" "What could we have done differently?"
- Thank participants for their time and effort.

Follow Up After the Alignment Meeting

- Follow up on assigned tasks and keep the group informed of progress.

3. A Quality Checklist for an Alignment Meeting

The following questions serve as a check to ensure your alignment meeting is getting at critical issues around role clarity, mutual support, and promises of business results.

Business Focus Statements

- Does each individual's business focus statement capture the unique value proposition of his or her role?
- Is there a strong level of synergy among business focus statements?
- Does each support the achievement of the leaders' business focus statement?

Operational Accountabilities

- Are some operational accountabilities unclaimed, or do some overlap? (If so, single-point accountabilities will need to be developed.)
- Do some operational accountabilities require further clarity? (If so, ask the individual in question to re-write the accountability following the alignment meeting.)

Leadership Accountabilities

- Do each member's leadership accountabilities support the type of work environment that the leader is trying to achieve?
- Does the overall set of leadership accountabilities send a clear, consistent, and supportive message to the organization?

Support Requirements

- Is the combined impact of all requests for support from any one individual, reasonable? (Discuss requests that cannot be met, then commit to providing the agreed level of support on those that can be fulfilled.)
- Are revisions to any individual's operational accountabilities or goals required, as a result of agreements that have been reached around the level of support that he or she has agreed to provide?

Goals

- Are each group member's goals aligned with the leader's goals?
- Are the goals measurable or observable, and time-based?
- Referring back to the operational accountabilities, are any other goals required?

Sustainment Plan

- Is there agreement on a practical sustainment plan for the workgroup? For example, an annual timetable for 'execution review meetings' with the group to review material changes to accountabilities; discuss progress on goals; and update support requirements.

4. The Alignment Discussion Guide

An alignment discussion guide organizes information from each group member's Accountability Agreement by category, thereby facilitating discussion of gaps, overlaps, and interdependencies. Rather than discussing one Accountability Agreement at a time, the 'alignment discussion guide' aids the group in discussing one entire area of accountability at a time, and each individual's accountability within this one area. As a result, groups accomplish more in a shorter period of meeting time.

Business focus statements are taken from each member's Accountability Agreement and presented on a spreadsheet for discussion.

Support requirements are presented on a separate spreadsheet, organized by the individual whose support is being requested.

Operational accountabilities, leadership accountabilities, and goals are also shown on separate spreadsheets, but organized by category. These are temporary categories for the purpose of the alignment discussion, and are created from a quick analysis of all the Accountability Agreements in the workgroup.

Business Focus Statements

Place the leader's business focus statement in the top left column then list each group member's business focus statement as shown in the example below.

Example:

Business Focus Statements – Power Group

John Smith, VP Power	Joe Thom, Director Hydro Assets	Toni Orr, Manager PR
The ongoing profitability of the Situ Plant in a safe and environmentally responsible manner.	The net contribution of MS Hydro assets to position ourselves for future growth opportunities.	Community and regulatory support for our current and proposed operations.
Fred Jones, Manager Generation	Sarah Smart, Director UK Ops	Murray Light, Manager HR
Profitable growth through leveraging our generation systems and processes.	Profitable expansion of our UK coal and hydro assets.	An organizational culture and HR systems that engage employees in the Company's success.
George Roads, Manager Finance	Dave Fields, Manager Plants	Sam Sampson, Manager IT
Quality financial information and expertise to improve financial returns for the BXR.	Fuel that creates maximum value for existing and future coal-fired generation plants.	Asset performance through technical support, strategic capital, and maintenance investments.

Operational Accountabilities

Categories are used to organize operational accountabilities. The category name is listed at the top left as a reference (e.g., business planning). Operational accountabilities corresponding to the category in question are then listed as shown in the example below. Needless to say, these categories are created from an analysis of all the operational accountabilities in the workgroup, and will therefore vary considerably from one workgroup to another.

Example:

Operational Accountabilities

Category: Business Planning and Strategy Development

John Smith, VP Power	Joe Thom, Director Hydro Assets	Toni Orr, Manager PR
5 year business plan for the Goldsmith Plant.	N/A	Execution strategy that aligns the team to the project's objectives.
Fred Jones, Manager Generation	**Sarah Smart, Director UK Ops**	**Murray Light, Manager HR**
2–5 year strategy and implementation plan that optimizes Generation's portfolio.	Strategy processes and plans documented and updated regularly.	A 5-year plan, including targets and actions that the GBX team uses to guide planning and execution.
George Roads, Manager Finance	**Dave Fields, Manager Plants**	**Sam Sampson, Manager IT**
Fuel exploited based on integrated economic plans for mine and plant value (e.g., long-term mine plans).	Long-term strategic investment plan (e.g., capital and planned maintenance).	Asset performance through technical support, strategic capital, and maintenance investments.

Leadership Accountabilities

Time goes by very quickly in the alignment meeting, and there is not usually time to discuss leadership accountabilities in detail. Suffice it to say that these need to be reviewed quickly to ensure they are not at cross purposes, and that everyone in the group is aligned on the work culture, leadership, and team practices that need to be supported to ensure workgroup success.

Support Requirements

Support requirements are organized in terms of the support requests that are being made of each individual. A spreadsheet is presented for each group member, showing the requests for support that are being made of that member, by all the other members of the group.

Example:

Support Requirements of John Smith, VP Power

Joe Thom, Director Hydro Assets	*Toni Orr, Manager PR*	*Fred Jones, Manager Generation*
• Sounding board for experience, decisions, reality checks • Assistance with manpower and materials when required • Heads up on emerging issues	• Immediate feedback and ongoing coaching on my behavior and the achievement (or lack of achievement) on my accountabilities • Continue to be accessible on short-term notice	• Cabinet solidarity around agreed Power decisions • Seek out my advice and involve me in business issues • Continue to be open to my challenge and feedback
Sarah Smart, Director UK Ops	*Murray Light, Manager HR*	*George Roads, Manager Finance*
• Business Unit involvement in strategic and execution planning	• Resources (e.g., staff, money, logistics, time) • Continue to cooperate and work with me on key business issues affecting my area	• Honest and open feedback about the finance function • Clear articulation of business objectives • Adherence to standards (e.g., safety, execution)
Dave Fields, Manager Plants	*Sam Sampson, Manager IT*	
• Timely information on business issues and challenges you are facing • Work collaboratively with me and my team	• Challenge me and each other, and provide me and each other with regular feedback.	

Goals

Like operational accountabilities, goals are organized by category for discussion. List the leader's goals first, to the right of the category name, then list each group member's goals as they relate to the category in question.

Example of Format:

Category X	Leader	Person A	Person B	Person C	Person D	Person E
	The leader's goals related to category X	Person A's goals related to category X	Person B's goals related to category X	Person C's goals related to category X	Person D's goals related to category X	Person E's goals related to category X
Category Y	The leader's goals related to category Y	Person A's goals related to category Y	Person B's goals related to category Y	Person C's goals related to category Y	Person D's goals related to category Y	Person E's goals related to category Y

Sustainment Plan

Each member's sustainment plan needs to be aligned, as sustainment is largely a workgroup activity. For example, the group might agree to review progress on accountabilities and goals quarterly, and to update and realign Accountability Agreements semi-annually.

Positive Consequences

Positive consequences are between an individual and his or her immediate supervisor. These are not made public, and are not discussed at an alignment meeting.

Chapter 8

Implementing the Accountability/Alignment

Process

THIS CHAPTER DESCRIBES HOW TO GET STARTED, once the decision has been made to implement Accountability/Alignment. Since not every person is immediately willing to embrace the required behavior, an assessment of organizational readiness is a vital part of an effective implementation strategy. This will help to ensure that good intentions and effort are not wasted.

Organizational Readiness

Accountability is one of those concepts that people think they understand until they try to use it. It gets confused with blame and stalled through a false association with punishment. Mischief results when such a concept, poorly understood, is hastily implemented. For example, a large financial organization called us because they had been working with Accountability Agreements for several months, and were not seeing any real benefit. The problem was that they were merely sending out copies of our book with a note attached, and requesting that people write their own Accountability Agreements. The result was simply a bunch of documents created in a spirit of compliance, an effort far too feeble to be useful.

Most skilled people are eager to be accountable. They are open to working with Accountability/Alignment if they have a sense of confidence in the organization itself, and feel that they can trust management with their genuine aspirations. People also need a sense of self-efficacy and reason to believe that they can make a difference in the organization. Finally, and perhaps most importantly, people are ready to be accountable when they have a sense of personal commitment to the organization's mission and success.

At his leadership workshops, Jim Kouzes sometimes shows a picture of a group of Peace Corps volunteers carrying heavy bags on their heads, crossing a tropical river, and up to their necks in mud. "Look closely at their faces," he says. "Yes, they are smiling. They are being richly rewarded by their own sense of mission."[6]

Another example of self-efficacy and personal obligation comes from Barbara, a client of ours. She had just begun reading our first book (*Accountability: Getting a Grip on Results*) when she received an email from a colleague. The email advised that the colleague was going to be late delivering a key piece of data to Barbara. This meant that Barbara would not be able to deliver a promised report to her manager by week's end. Here's what happened, in Barbara's own words:

> I would usually just apologize to my boss and tell him that he would have the report sometime next week. This time, I thought, this is what happens around here all the time. So, I called my colleague and told him I was accountable for getting this report to my boss by Friday, with no excuses. I asked him how I could support him in getting the data to me on time. Surprisingly, he was very responsive. He got the information to me later that day, and I met my accountability to my boss. I said to myself, I'm only on page 29. By the time I finish this book I'm going to be a terror around here!

Deciding Where to Start

Accountability/Alignment works best as a system-wide change process. It starts with a renewed strategic orientation to each individual's role, along with a commitment by each person to fulfill his or her individual business bargain. This can contribute to a 'step level' improvement in the work environment, teamwork, and business results. Given such possibility, the question becomes: "Where to start?"

We see four options to try and one to avoid:

- When possible, start at the top (with the CEO and executive team).
- When appropriate, cascade the process top-down throughout the organization, one level at a time.
- Start with influential leaders — those people who will be able to encourage and support others to adopt Accountability/Alignment once it has proven valuable to them personally and to their workgroups.
- Start with yourself (a deep appreciation and personal modeling of this process will enable you to champion its implementation throughout the organization).

John Kotter's process for leading change:

1. *Establish a sense of urgency*
2. *Establish a steering committee*
3. *Establish a vision and strategy*
4. *Communicate and model the change*
5. *Approach the change systemically*
6. *Seek out and recognize small wins*
7. *Use current success as a lever*
8. *Make the new way 'normal'*

John Kotter, *Leading Change*

Write Your Own Accountability Agreement

Invest 3 hours of your time with a consultant who is experienced in helping people to rethink and reframe their roles. Share your Accountability Agreement with others — your direct reports, your boss, your peers. Then, tune up your Accountability Agreement based on their feedback. The clarity and positive business results that follow will speak for themselves. Next, arrange for others in your workgroup to write their individual Accountability Agreements, and then to align these agreements within the workgroup. It is during and following the alignment process that the value of Accountability/Alignment is fully captured. Innovators know that good ideas inspire others, and that enthusiasm is contagious.

- Don't start with extremely traditional managers or difficult workgroups (save them for later, after the process has proven its value with other groups in the organization).

Where Extra Effort May Be Required

Some groups may, at first glance, find it difficult to fully accept a process aimed at articulating and tracking accountability across the organization. In preparation for implementing Accountability/Alignment, it is useful to acknowledge that the following groups will initially require extra attention and support:

- frontline employees
- employees in large traditional bureaucracies
- managers who are unfamiliar with modern leadership practices
- people who fear being accountable
- people for whom the organization is not a priority

The following provides guidance when implementing Accountability/ Alignment with each of these groups.

Frontline Employees

Strategic thinking is a relatively new skill for many frontline employees who have spent their careers in operating units. Yet, these employees often excel at goal setting and getting things done. And, once they have been coached through developing their own accountabilities and have aligned these within their workgroup, they often become strong advocates for working with a broader business perspective. They appreciate knowing how their efforts fit into the 'bigger picture.'

Employees in Large Traditional Bureaucracies

Employees in large bureaucracies — despite working very hard as many of them often do — sometimes feel that their ability to influence is very limited. They often feel unable to plan in terms of results for their customers or those for whom they provide services. However, we have seen many successful examples of accountability in such large organizations, as long as there is support for Accountability/Alignment from senior leaders at the executive level or within a given department.

Managers Unfamiliar with Modern Leadership Practices

Even today, some managers are unfamiliar with contemporary leadership practices. Their thinking equates responsibility with authority, and discounts the importance of individual initiative. It is foolhardy and impossible, they would argue, to be accountable for an outcome that you cannot *fully* and authoritatively control. This worldview implies that accountability must parallel hierarchy. In most of today's interdependent organizations, where no one has full control yet all have significant opportunity to influence, this set of beliefs is no longer tenable.

The challenge is to help such managers understand the importance of and adopt more current leadership practices. This might involve training or coaching before implementing Accountability/Alignment within their workgroup.

People who Fear 'Being Accountable'

Some people, for a variety of reasons, simply do not want to be held accountable — or to hold themselves accountable. They prefer being told what to do, and even how to do it, and then being closely supervised as they work. Such people could not sleep at night if they had to be accountable for a business outcome. They may be highly risk averse, they may have been conditioned over many years to 'just do your job,' or they might have little emotional attachment to their work or employer. Out of insecurity or fear, they seek employment with few demands. The organization needs to encourage and develop such individuals to be accountable, where they have the potential for making a greater contribution.

People for Whom the Organization is not a Priority

Finally, there are perfectly healthy, mature, and accountable people who will have different degrees of commitment to their work, and to the organization that employs them. For some, their work will always be a lower priority than other aspects of their lives. Poor performers and dishonest employees are relatively easy to recognize (if you're paying attention), but it is an additional challenge to deal with people whose interest is in adequacy, not excellence. Despite having all your organizational ducks in a row (clear goals, trust, empowerment, honest people, and so on), and despite possessing desirable personal qualities like reliability and competence, such people only seem interested in meeting the acceptable standard, not beating it.

Approaches to improving their performance can involve aligning their interests with those of the organization through rewards or incentive programs. Alternatively, an organization can simply accept them as they are, for the steady contribution they make. If an organization has created a culture of complacency it may be important to develop a long term staffing strategy, starting with a review of hiring and retention policies to ensure that the entire workforce is not being geared toward mediocrity. It is essential to align strategy and staffing so that people are able and willing to take the organization where it wants to go. The Accountability/Alignment process raises such issues for executive resolution.

Integrate Accountability/Alignment with Related Business Systems in the Organization

A key implementation step involves integrating and positioning Accountability/Alignment in relation to other processes in the organization, such as performance management, the compensation system, and quality assurance processes. It is important to consider what predictable friction points likely exist where these processes interconnect, and how these frictions might be resolved. An organization-wide approach for ensuring that business processes are aligned can add discipline and remove wasteful inconsistency.

Great Excuses for Why Accountability Won't Work[7]

The following will help you identify, challenge, and overcome dodges to implementing accountability in your organization.

Excuse 1: I can't be accountable without full control or authority.

The 'right to give orders' has largely been replaced by the necessity to innovate, network, and exercise influence. Accountability needs to be omnidirectional in modern organizations.

Excuse 2: Our organization uses a number of traditional approaches and wouldn't want to change.

Much of what knowledge workers produce cannot be defined in job descriptions or competency profiles. Conceptualizing opportunities and devising creative solutions requires initiative and commitment. You can't generate this from a list of tasks or behaviors.

Excuse 3: I don't have the time; anyway, things change too quickly around here.

Everyone has exactly the same amount of time — what varies are people's priorities. The faster things change, the more important it is to understand your piece of the business and what other people expect you to deliver.

Excuse 4: Promises get broken all the time; it's no big deal.

People need to expect more from themselves and from each other. Excuses don't work where there are clear individual accountabilities that are reviewed regularly within the workgroup.

Excuse 5: I don't know what my boss wants, so I can't be accountable.

This is roughly equivalent of that old phrase: "Just tell me what to do, boss." Subservience and lack of individual initiative are out of place at any level in modern organizations. Empowerment and accountability are inseparable.

Excuse 6: My job is too complex to be described in terms of accountabilities.

This statement demonstrates a problem of perspective and confusion about outcomes. Lofty statements such as "I'll do my best," however well intentioned, are hollow.

Excuse 7: My job is simple and obvious, so there is no need to think strategically about my role.

Simple and non-accountable jobs are now rare. Almost everyone now needs to think strategically about his or her contribution, and operate as if they are running their own personal business within the organization.

Excuse 8: My boss would only use it against me.

An employee might fear that a clearly articulated Accountability Agreement could become a trap, and sadly, in some organizations this may be true. Enlightened leaders focus on success, not on failure, blame, or punishment.

Excuse 9: This will have to wait until my boss gets on board.

In most organizations, many individuals have some potential to innovate, to initiate personal change, and to exercise leadership. Innovators know that good ideas can inspire others, and that enthusiasm is contagious.

Early Wins are the Key

We hope the suggestions provided here will help you successfully launch any improvement initiative, including Accountability/Alignment. Getting off on the right foot greatly facilitates ongoing implementation. Early success helps to overcome skepticism and builds credibility. The key is to celebrate 'early wins' wherever you choose to begin, and then to use these to build momentum as implementation proceeds across the organization.

Chapter 9

Accountability/Alignment in Daily Practice

ONCE IMPLEMENTED AND ALIGNED, individual Accountability Agreements need to be kept current and maintained to facilitate the achievement of business results. They must continue to accurately reflect those critical everyday conversations that generate trust, encourage problem solving instead of blaming, and allow people to genuinely engage their talents in the service of the organization.

Time needs to be built into workgroup meetings for round table reporting and discussion on how each individual is doing on his or her accountabilities and goals, and to discuss the level of support being provided. Accordingly, this chapter reviews ways of capturing the value of Accountability/Alignment within organizations through everyday use, execution review, and updating and realigning.

Everyday Use

Aligned Accountability Agreements contribute to everyday organizational effectiveness in many ways. In addition to guiding individual action and aligning workgroup roles and goals, these agreements facilitate organizational change and conflict resolution. They also guide Human Resource initiatives such as staffing, recruiting, orientation, and coaching programs.

Supporting Change

Accountability/Alignment helps organizations to be more agile and adaptable to changing circumstances. Since an individual's accountabilities and goals are linked to larger organizational goals, people have a license for pushing change within their area of accountability. In this way, Accountability/Alignment provides a context for empowerment and encourages frontline people to suggest and initiate innovative ways to satisfy the customers that they deal with directly every day. Frontline people know the customer best, and have a lot to contribute beyond their daily role. In addition, as alignment crosses functional lines, it helps make connections that otherwise might not happen, and provides needed understanding and support for system-wide change within the organization. Finally, clear accountabilities tailored to the current organizational context, and to the individual's unique strengths help remove the complexity associated with change, and focus action on the few critical tasks that are likely to yield the greatest return.

Resolving Conflict

Accountability Agreements provide a context and a logical process for legitimizing dialogue, surfacing assumptions, clarifying expectations, and agreeing on mutual support requirements. Adult-to-adult negotiation takes place with discussion based on a clear and common understanding of individual roles and expectations.

Facilitating Staffing Decisions

Staffing decisions are made more transparent as the Accountability Agreement demonstrates the 'business need' for a given role. It does this by making the business outcomes expected from the new role abundantly clear, and thereby more easily discussed and challenged.

Recruiting Employees

Knowing the end results that a jobholder must deliver assists in identifying suitable candidates for transfer or promotion into that position. By way of example, a school board in a large city recently used an Accountability Agreement to guide the process for recruiting a new Superintendent of Schools. The Accountability Agreement was written to reflect ideal outcomes expected from the role, and was helpful in attracting and selecting the right individual.

New Employee Orientation

Accountability/Alignment enables new people to get up-to-speed and begin contributing quickly in the organization by giving them a full, clear, and aligned perspective of their role. It also serves as a vehicle to ensure a smooth handoff when assuming a role from another person. Without the leverage provided by a tool such as Accountability/Alignment, new people are often slow to make a full contribution due to common corporate assumptions such as the need to 'pay your dues' before you earn the right to be heard.

Coaching and Mentoring

An Accountability Agreement provides a disciplined process and a structured framework for both support and challenge during coaching.

Execution Review

Effective execution demands ongoing follow up, and can't be taken for granted. A regular execution review meeting or phone conference is essential to ensure that the organization is on track with its strategic objectives, and gains ongoing value from the Accountability/Alignment process. In this way, the process is incorporated into workgroup practice and becomes part of the organization's way of doing business. Bossidy, Charan, and Burck provide an excellent example of an informal, monthly 'execution review' conference call:

> Starting at the highest levels, Brown (referring to Richard Brown, CEO at EDS) created new ways to drive accountability and collaboration. In the monthly 'performance call,' for example, he, his COO, and the CFO began hosting Monday morning conference calls with the company's roughly top 150 leaders. These calls are essentially an ongoing operating review ... The talk is straightforward, even blunt, designed to elicit truth and coach people in the behavior Brown expects of his managers. 'Intense candor,' Brown calls it, 'a balance of optimism and motivation with realism ... The calls can be uncomfortable for those in the negative column. In front of their peers, executives have to explain why and what

they're doing to get back on track ... But just by the fact that it happens, human nature says you want to be one of the ones doing well.'[8]

Meeting Process

As part of the execution review meeting, each group member briefly reviews progress — or lack thereof — toward achieving his or her accountabilities and goals, and invites discussion within the workgroup. In this way, the level of progress is briefly reviewed for each individual's accountabilities and goals, along with the effect of such progress on the accountabilities and goals held by others in the workgroup. Support requirements are also discussed as a way of ensuring that current requirements for support are adequate and realistic, and that others are delivering on the support they have promised to each individual. Action plans are agreed in order to overcome difficulties and guide progress. The key to ongoing success is that the execution review meeting be focused on results and progress. As discussed in Chapter 4, this is best achieved via a process of dialogue, learning, challenge, and support — not judging and blaming.

What Execution Review 'Is' and 'Is Not'

This is a business meeting not an appraisal meeting. Accountability/ Alignment provides the needed structure for execution review to become a real exercise in leadership, with meaningful dialogue and workgroup learning, rather than just a series of formal reports.

Some form of annual performance evaluation by the workgroup leader is still required. However, by using self-assessments, the execution review process remains free of the usual awkwardness, positioning, and procrastination so often associated with traditional performance evaluation.

Updating and Realigning

As circumstances change, Accountability Agreements will need to be updated and then realigned within the workgroup. In most organizations, given the rapid pace of change, the update and realignment meeting will likely need to occur every six months, and in exceptional circumstances, even more frequently. Exceptional conditions that may trigger the need for an update and realignment meeting are outlined in Chapter 11.

Don't Let It Atrophy

The moment any new idea or process is ignored or allowed to atrophy, people will infer that it is no longer important, and that it can safely be ignored. This applies just as much to Accountability/Alignment as to any other change initiative. Survival of the fittest does not necessarily apply to good ideas in organizations. More than 500 years ago, Machiavelli wryly observed: "... there is nothing more difficult to execute, nor more dubious of success, nor more dangerous to administer than to introduce a new system of things."[9] This observation still holds true. Good ideas are not necessarily retained in organizations, and they don't necessarily continue to grow despite their potential. As a matter of experience, others will sometimes oppose a process precisely because it demands change in the organization. Change always involves a loss of some kind, even though this might be something as basic as the loss of a familiar way of working.

Russell Ackoff was fond of saying that 'good ideas have legs' — that good ideas will always move ahead. This is only half true. Good ideas can also be threatening, and are often resisted for a myriad of reasons. Accordingly, good processes need champions, people who will regularly demonstrate the business value of the process, influence others to persevere despite the 'pockets of resistance,' and work hard to ensure the long-term contribution of the process to organization success.

> *Jim Collins, author of* Good to Great, *suggests four ways of leading discussions so that facts are confronted and dealt with honestly in organizations.*
>
> • *Lead with questions, not answers*
> • *Engage in dialogue and debate, not coercion*
> • *Conduct autopsies, without blame*
> • *Build red flag mechanisms that turn information into information that cannot be ignored*

Harnessing the Accountability/Alignment Process to Achieve Business Results

Banks like payments more than promises. No matter how impressive words may be, merely saying something in itself delivers nothing. Organizations need strong follow up mechanisms to ensure that people are getting the support they require, are delivering on promised business results, and are being recognized and rewarded for success.

Although many people can generate promising ideas, not everyone will be prepared to do the hard work of putting their ideas into action. As Tom Peters says, many neuroscientists have the talent to become Nobel Laureates, but only a few are willing to do the hard work of slicing mice brains, day after day, to achieve the necessary research results. Each workgroup leader can ensure that potential of improvement initiatives such as Accountability/Alignment are harnessed to actually achieve the intended results. This usually means applying some discipline, in this case, the discipline of execution review meetings, and update and realignment meetings. Harvesting the value of change initiatives is not complicated, but it does take commitment, discipline, and a relentless focus on results.

Part III

Sustaining the Process

PART III OFFERS A DEEPER LOOK AT THE THINKING UNDERLYING THE OPERATING PRINCIPLES OF ACCOUNTABILITY AND ALIGNMENT.™

We then look at how the value of this process can be assessed, and how to sustain this or any other improvement process over the long term.

Chapter 10

The Roots of Accountability/Alignment

NOW THAT WE HAVE COVERED THE BASICS OF Accountability/ Alignment and the operating principles underlying this process, it is time to go deeper and examine the roots of this approach. In doing so, we explore the fundamental nature of accountability, and the organizational context that is necessary for Accountability/Alignment to bear fruit.

Learnings from Practice

The following learnings lie at the root of the operating principles of accountability and alignment discussed in Chapters 2 and 3.

The Fundamental Nature of Accountability

- Accountability is an individual fact
- While accountability can be delegated, it is always retained
- Accountabilities are never shared at the same level in an organization
- Although not shared, leadership accountabilities (as distinct from operational accountabilities) are often 'held in common'
- Accountability does not require full control
- Accountability does not imply infallibility
- Accountability only works with the willing

The Necessary Context of Accountability/Alignment

- Accountability/Alignment requires an ethical context
- Leadership accountabilities extend beyond simple economic success
- Accountability is not a substitute for leadership
- Focus on 'accountable for,' not 'accountable to'
- Successful implementation is not the same as sustainment
- Organizations continue to learn about accountability over many years

The Fundamental Nature of Accountability

The following insights inform the first and most basic operating principle of accountability (i.e., accountability is personal and not shared at the same level in an organization).

Accountability is an Individual Fact

A client of ours jokingly uses the term, 'single neck accountability.' It's funny because it's partly true. When accountability is perceived as something shared, even between just two people, it is diluted and dissipates. Workgroups, committees, or any collection of people cannot be personally answerable. While a group member will hold specific accountabilities for business results within the group, only the group's leader, as an individual, is fully accountable for the success or failure of the group, as a whole, to deliver on its overall mandate (we examine accountability in teams more deeply in Chapter 14).

The willingness to accept full responsibility — that is, to be accountable for all the implications of our actions — grows directly out of accepting the fact of our free will.

Peter Koestenbaum and Peter Block,
Freedom and Accountability at Work

Accountability Has to be Learned[10]

Children are not born accountable. They are, of necessity, dependent. When a six-year-old spills his milk, he will say something like: "Mom, it got spilt," but not: "Mom, I spilled it." And an adult who says: "That's just the way I am" is not creating an acceptable reason for thoughtless behavior. Nor is it even an accurate description. Since the time of Aristotle, leading thinkers have maintained that the choices we make determine what we become. Sydney Harris[11] notes: "We have not passed that subtle line between childhood and adulthood until we move from the passive voice to the active voice. That is, until we stop saying 'the file got lost,' and instead say, 'I lost the file.'"

While Accountability Can be Delegated, it is Always Retained

A leader is accountable for the success of people who report directly to him or her, and for the achievements or mistakes made by these direct reports. As an example, Ms. Jones, a senior manager, assigns accountability for the success of a key project to one of her direct reports. While the 'direct report' in question is now accountable for project success, so too is Ms. Jones. Whether the project succeeds or fails, Ms. Jones' made the decision to delegate this project, and she chose the person to be accountable for project success. These decisions are a reflection of the quality of her managerial judgment and the exercise of her accountability.

An example from personal life may be where you decide to turn the management of all your investments over to a financial advisor. The short-term benefit is that you do not have to be personally involved in managing your own investments. In the long term, your financial security will strengthen or weaken based on decisions made by your financial advisor; however, you cannot escape your accountability for the selection of the advisor.

Accountabilities are Never Shared 'at the Same Level' in an Organization

Although this point has been made in Chapter 2, it is so important, and so frequently misunderstood that we want to mention it again, just briefly. A CEO is personally accountable for everything that happens in the organization. Having said this, we know that for practical purposes, the CEO's accountabilities must be assigned to others, throughout the organization. Thus, while the CEO and a Vice-President may hold some of the same accountabilities, they are at different reporting levels in the organization. However, no two Vice-Presidents at the same level in an organization would hold the same accountabilities. The Vice-Presidents, in turn, would likely assign some of their accountabilities to others, and so on.

Occasionally we see groups of people at the same level performing similar roles within a given department (e.g., lawyers, engineers, land negotiators). While such individuals may well describe their accountabilities in a similar way, their accountabilities relate to different parts of the business, different areas, different customers, different portfolios, and the like. The essential notion of 'single point' accountability remains intact.

Although Not Shared, Leadership Accountabilities (as distinct from Operational Accountabilities) are Often 'Held in Common'

Operational accountabilities focus on the 'what,' or the business outcomes that are being sought, while leadership accountabilities focus on the 'how,' or the context in which work is performed. Thus, leadership accountabilities focus on the organization's work environment or culture, including the values espoused by leaders, leadership practices, and teamwork. It is therefore likely, and even desirable, that several leaders aspire to identical or similar leadership accountabilities, for example, 'a leadership style that motivates staff and instills a sense of urgency.' Nonetheless, each individual leader is personally accountable for achieving this result. We encourage leaders to avoid language that suggests accountability can be shared — be it an operational or leadership accountability.

Accountability Does Not Require Full Control

Accountability is unconditional and is not a function of control. For example, a senior Vice-President of Human Resources described his business focus statement as, 'an organizational culture and HR systems that ensure our people are fully engaged in the Company's success.' Needless to say, a Senior Vice-President does not have full control over all aspects of an organization's culture. Neither does a CEO, for that matter. But organizational culture can be strongly affected by effective leadership and the application of practical tools. Accomplishing such an outcome requires alignment of interests, strong mutual support, and skill in exerting significant levels of influence across the organization.

Accountability Does Not Imply Infallibility

Accountability does not require that people be infallible. There will be instances where an individual is able to show that he or she did everything possible — and still, due to circumstances that were beyond prediction, influence, or control, was not able to fully deliver on a promised business result. Leaders need to understand these reasons, and not take an unthinking, uncaring, or arbitrary approach, or automatically label these shortfalls as 'failures.' To refuse to accept such reasons is to refuse to regard the individual as a moral agent; for it is in the nature of moral agents (human beings) that their best efforts will sometimes fall short of desired results.

Similarly, this does not mean that the individual in question should expect to share in unearned rewards. Nonetheless, in a fair business bargain, it is essential to recognize that the individual has the right to expect support and respect for having taken initiative, kept people informed, exercised due diligence, and done all that was possible under the circumstances.

Accountability Only Works with the Willing

Just as 'you can lead a horse to water but you can't make him drink,' there is no way that accountability can be forced on people. If imposed instead of nurtured, Accountability/Alignment, like any improvement initiative, will simply become another clever and cynical game. A basic principle here is that 'leaders go first'. As others see that Accountability/Alignment is worthwhile, they will become more inclined to

> *The idea that we are authors of our actions is required by morality.*
>
> John Gray, *Straw Dogs*

Accountability vs. Responsibility: A Distinction without a Worthwhile Difference

We are often asked to discuss the difference between the terms 'accountability' and 'responsibility.' Some argue that only managers are accountable, whereas front-line employees are responsible. The idea here is that managers are accountable for achieving business outcomes, whereas employees are only responsible for doing what they are told to do.[12] We believe it is a mistake to create two such classes of employees, where the implication is that accountability rests solely with managers. Such a distinction perpetuates a parent-child mindset, creates confusion and draws people into low-yield discussions about the difference in principle between the two words. For our practical purposes, the terms 'accountability' and 'responsibility' are synonymous.

adopt the process for themselves and their workgroups. The organizational conditions and processes required to generate accountability require an environment of integrity and trust. In the same way that you can't get a plant to grow with coercion or force, accountability will develop best when nurtured, encouraged, and given time to prove its worth.

The Necessary Context of Accountability/Alignment

Where the following elements are in place, Accountability/Alignment is likely to flourish and provide value for the organization over many years.

Accountability/Alignment Requires an Ethical Context

Accountability/Alignment fits where there is a commitment to transparency, since it requires the open sharing of Accountability Agreements and good faith negotiation of mutual support. In such an environment, it is unlikely that deception can take root.

Leadership Accountabilities Extend Beyond Economic Success

John Gray argues that: "where people hold community sacred, it is an affront to put prosperity in competition with community."[13] Humans are not just economic animals, and the implications of accountability go beyond organizational production and financial prosperity. Accordingly, when the organization becomes a main social element in people's lives, it must respect and not just exploit employees' feelings of attachment. Leadership accountabilities are essential here. This is where each individual commits to the human *and* organizational conditions necessary for achieving business results. These include management and leadership practices, working relationships and teamwork, work environment and organizational culture, and the organization's relationship with the communities in which it operates.

Accountability is Not a Substitute for Leadership

The notion of accountability, and more specifically, the process we call Accountability/Alignment, helps leaders organize and control at a higher level than does direct supervision — at the level of organizational values, purpose, and goals. This does not mean direct supervision is unnecessary, but does recognize its limitations in modern organizations. Certainly, the more people's interests are aligned with those of the organization, the less need there will be to regularly supervise their work.

> *Kouzes and Posner, authors of* The Leadership Challenge, *suggest that enlightened leaders:*
>
> - *Challenge the process*
> - *Inspire a shared vision*
> - *Enable others to act*
> - *Model the way*
> - *Encourage the heart*

Focus on 'Accountable For' Not 'Accountable To'

Talking in terms of 'accountable for' — as opposed to 'accountable to' — keeps discussion focused on desired results, rather than on hierarchy. The moment you start talking in terms of 'accountable to,' it becomes quite possible to confuse the outcomes being sought with the necessary reporting relationships of the organization (e.g., job titles, formal authority). The mischief embedded in focusing primarily on 'accountable to' is illustrated by a presentation one of us attended in Russia. A Russian consultant claiming to have gained great insight into Western styles of management stated: "There are three principles I have learned from studying Western methods of management. The first principle is that the customer is always right. The second principle is that your boss is your most important customer. The third principle is obvious." When such an approach is adopted, even tacitly, any appeal for employee commitment becomes an equally bad joke.

Successful Implementation is Not the Same as Sustainment

We cannot overstress the issue of sustainment with client organizations. Groups are often very pleased with themselves following completion of their Accountability Agreements and the alignment process — and well they should be. Yet it is important that this not be seen as the end of their effort. The process has just been installed. Now it must be maintained so that it can continue to enhance organizational results.

Organizations Continue to Learn About Accountability Over Many Years

Not surprisingly, there is an inevitable learning curve involved in working with Accountability/Alignment. Many of our clients have initially seen the process as something familiar — often as an improved form of performance management. Then, once they begin working with the process, they sometimes see it as a simple recipe: complete Accountability Agreements, align within workgroups, review regularly — they project a 'checklist mentality' onto what they are beginning to learn.

However, as our clients become more familiar with this work, they come to see its potential to positively reconstruct the culture of the organization, including improvements in people's 'line of sight' to corporate strategy and how they work across departments to ensure mutual support and teamwork. Continuing success connects the process with even deeper values. Over time, Accountability/Alignment becomes central to helping organizations realize and sustain not only productivity, but also transparency and reliable ethical practice across their organizations.

Action Learning

The concept of action learning[14] — doing something, evaluating results, learning from the experience, then doing it even better in the next learning cycle — is helpful when working with Accountability/Alignment. As a consulting company, we also continue to learn — along with our clients — about accountability and to improve our Accountability/ Alignment process. By consistently reviewing key learnings, leaders accelerate their understanding and use of Accountability/Alignment, and through this, the ability to help their organizations to continuously improve their business results.

Chapter 11

The Operating Principles of Achievement

OVER THE PAST TWENTY YEARS, managers have been engaged in many extensive efforts to improve the functioning of their organizations. The list is fairly long: T-groups, Quality Circles, Transactional Analysis, Zero Based Budgeting, and Process Reengineering, among many others.

Most of these initiatives have left a legacy of value in one form or another. For example, group participation in decision-making was first introduced in the form of Quality Circles, and Reengineering has left an awareness of the importance of streamlining and aligning business processes. But the sad fact remains that most of these improvement efforts did not have the lasting impact they might have had.

This unfortunate pattern of outcomes is not inevitable. The following 'operating principles of achievement' will guide you in ensuring lasting value from any organizational improvement initiative — especially Accountability/Alignment. These six principles are predicated on our experience, and on the diverse yet congruent literature of organizational learning and personal habit change.[15]

The Operating Principles of Achievement

1. Accountability/Alignment becomes the vehicle for aligning roles
2. Accountability Agreements are used regularly to organize work
3. Accountability Agreements are updated and realigned regularly
4. Leaders model accountable and aligned behavior
5. The process is used to complement existing practices
6. The process is audited and continuously improved

Operating Principle 1
Accountability/Alignment Becomes the Vehicle for Aligning Roles

The initiative and energy for Accountability/Alignment should come from the top — the CEO and senior executives. While HR groups may play a coordination role, any major business improvement process such as Accountability/Alignment needs to be owned and championed at the senior leadership and operating levels. When this happens, leaders across the organization understand that they have a central and ongoing role in modeling and sustaining this approach to achieving positive business results.

Operating Principle 2
Accountability Agreements are Used Regularly to Organize Work

The first key to ongoing success is to use Accountability Agreements to regularly guide workgroup discussion (we discussed execution review meetings in Chapter 9). The second is to keep Accountability Agreements up-to-date and visible within the organization. An example of the latter comes from a client organization. The senior executive group makes a point of reviewing the Accountability Agreements of their direct reports on a quarterly basis. This same group posted their own Accountability Agreements on the company's intranet. This also created incentive to keep their agreements current, and each time an executive's role changed, his or her Accountability Agreement was quickly updated and reposted to the intranet. Employees acted on this example, keeping their own Accountability Agreements up-to-date so that others could use them as a reliable reference document.

Operating Principle 3
Accountability Agreements are Updated and Realigned Regularly

As time passes and the initial excitement wanes, the practice in organizations regarding an improvement initiative often slides toward neglect. To counter this tendency, initiatives need to be re-energized and adapted as the life of the organization unfolds. This renewal and realigning is particularly critical after significant changes such as:

- a change in leadership or key personnel
- a sizeable change in workgroup membership
- a significant change in roles within the workgroup
- a shift in the organization's business environment
- a change in the organization's strategy
- a substantial conflict within a workgroup or across departments (this usually indicates the need for some realigning of individual accountabilities and goals)

Updating involves revising each group member's Accountability Agreement, while realigning involves workgroup discussion in order to:

- ensure relevance of each individual's accountabilities and goals to changing circumstances
- resolve any new gaps or overlaps of accountabilities or goals
- confirm interdependencies and support requirements, and ensure each individual is well positioned to fulfill his or her promises of business results

Operating Principle 4
Leaders Model Accountable and Aligned Behavior

A leader's power is proportional to his or her credibility. Leaders generate credibility by 'modeling the way'[16] — demonstrating personal accountability, and by personally using the Accountability/Alignment process.

The Essential Qualities of Accountable Leadership[17]

Leadership competence is less a function of technique than of personal integration and maturity of judgment. The accountable leader understands that for commitment to be present, people need to be informed, involved, allowed to influence, and ultimately given the right to choose accountability for themselves. Elements of leadership that are most critical to implementing Accountability/Alignment include:

1. Leaders Understand and Embrace the Importance of a Fair Deal

Creating a 'fair deal' for people at work releases human potential. Individuals are supported to exercise personal judgment and take ownership of business results.

2. Leaders Harness and Grow the Power of Alignment

By aligning effort and eliminating the bickering that wastes so much time in organizations, leaders help people focus on what is valued by the organization. Because they are not wasting effort on 'busyness,' people experience themselves as productive members of the business.

3. Leaders Focus on Results Rather than on Activities

Focusing on results encourages people to look outward toward their products and services, including the organization's place in the market. When results are emphasized, customers come into focus.

4. Leaders Encourage Ownership Rather than Compliance

Leadership is the art of getting others to want to do what needs to be done. Leaders shape people's views to care about the organization's purpose, to clearly see the connection between that purpose and their own enlightened self-interest, and to bring a stamp of personal pride to their work.

5. Leaders are Open to Learning Rather than Protecting an Image of Perfection

By way of example, where those involved with safety incidents are punished rather than encouraged to treat such events as learning opportunities, the risk-averse culture that emerges often leaves safety incidents unreported. On the other hand, where problems and mistakes can be discussed at the outset without blaming, it is less likely that schedules will slip or that targets will inexplicably be missed.

6. Leaders Rely on the Intelligence and Support of their People

Leaders encourage people to use judgment and discretion, and then hold them accountable for business results. They are open to learning from their employees, and can admit when they don't have the best answers. By allowing employees to demonstrate their own intelligence and capabilities, a positive self-fulfilling prophecy is set in place.

7. Leaders Play to Win, Rather than Simply Playing 'Not to Lose'

Leaders encourage people to look for the prize in a bigger game, rather than focusing on whether their actions are defensible or anxiously protecting a status quo. Projecting an optimistic view of the future creates courage — literally 'encourages.' A Russian colleague summed this up saying: "Leadership is the multiplication of hope."

Credibility gives leaders the power to rally others to a common cause, and to engage the 'discretionary efforts' of employees. Courageous leadership decisions are often hard to justify in foresight but always judged in hindsight. We worked with one CEO, who, after declaring that the organization was in financial trouble, suspended payment of a long-standing dividend, much to the outrage of many shareholders. He received threatening letters and a great deal of criticism in the business press for his decision. In the longer-term, however, he was proven right. The company regained its financial health and was able to reinstate the dividend. If he had not taken his original difficult decision, the company may not have been able to survive at all. He took accountability for 'returning the organization to financial health' and acted on this even though he initially stood alone.

Leading by example, especially in difficult times, is the most important execution benchmark for any process. Nothing 'sticks' without credible leadership. Without the inspiration, influence, and perseverance of credible leaders, good ideas are not necessarily implemented or retained — especially those requiring change.

Operating Principle 5
The Accountability/Alignment Process is Used to Complement Existing Practices

Certain failure comes from introducing an improvement initiative into a hostile or unreceptive environment. When beginning such an initiative, it is vital to consider whether it will be nurtured or stifled by the organization's current environment. Make sure that the organizational ground is fertile and prepared before planting the seeds of an improvement initiative. Then, protect the initiative as it grows until it can demonstrate its full value. For example, sustainment is greatly enhanced when efforts are made to ensure that Accountability/Alignment is used to complement existing people practices (e.g., teambuilding, performance management). When this is done well, the new initiative does not trigger the organization's immune response, and sustainment is much more likely.

Operating Principle 6
The Accountability/Alignment Process is Audited and Continuously Improved

Like any process, Accountability/Alignment needs to be regularly audited — we suggest annually — and continuously improved as part of organizational learning. A corporate Audit Department, perhaps using a tool such as a balanced scorecard,[18] can check for clear and aligned accountabilities as part of each audit they perform. If the value of an improvement initiative is never assessed with some form of audit, the tacit message is that it can be safely ignored.

Key Steps to Sustaining Accountability/Alignment

Based on the operating principles outlined above, the following steps are indispensable to sustaining Accountability/Alignment over the long term. First, designate a senior executive to actively champion the process. This requires someone who has the interest, influence, time, and commitment to ensure that the process is effectively operated and sustained across the organization. Second, provide ongoing coaching. Compare learning to use a management process such as Accountability/Alignment with learning to operate a piece of heavy equipment. We have no problem understanding that people need time to learn to operate equipment properly, yet we often short change people by not preparing and coaching them to use management processes properly. Third, implement a sustainment plan. This involves regularly 'tuning up' and realigning Accountability Agreements, and should include tracking, assessing, and reporting on the execution of Accountability/Alignment. It should also include the necessary adjustments to ensure ongoing value is being realized from this process.

Start with Sustainment in Mind

Sustaining a successful organizational improvement initiative is the most fulfilling — and least exciting — aspect of organizational change. Fulfillment comes from sustained results that you can be proud of over the long term. However, sustainment is least exciting because it is akin to the 'heavy lifting' of managerial work. It is difficult, sometimes discouraging, often frustrating, and rarely immediately rewarded. Novelty catches peoples'

> *Patience and tenacity of purpose are worth more than twice their weight of cleverness.*
>
> Thomas Henry Huxley (1825–95),
> English biologist.

attention, but ongoing execution and sustainment just looks like everyday work — and it is! Given this reality, we can only encourage perseverance. The lengthy roster of abandoned organizational change initiatives can mostly be attributed to a lack of follow through. Our advice is to pick a practical and proven approach such as Accountability/Alignment, and initiate it with sustainment in mind. In this way, you and your organization are much more likely to harvest the promise offered by such an improvement process.

Chapter 12

Measuring the Benefits

A S MODERN ORGANIZATIONS ARE DYNAMIC AND COMPLEX, many factors inevitably influence the success of an improvement initiative. Yet, all too often, these initiatives are judged only on a few prominent features — for example, some serendipitous change in an important business indicator. The problem is not that this approach is necessarily wrong, it's that it is incomplete and highly inferential. To assess the value of an improvement initiative with any certainty, you have to look beyond the dramatic positive or negative impressions, and consider three broad areas of evaluation. We call these areas *fit, formative,* and *final.*

Fit
(evaluation prior to implementation)
- Does the improvement initiative 'fit,' given the context of the current organization culture? Will the work environment support or impede the improvement initiative?

Formative
(evaluation during implementation)
- What are the indicators of success or failure during implementation?

Final
(evaluation following implementation)
- How did it go? Was it worth the effort and cost? What are the lasting gains?

These three areas of evaluation provide a complete picture of what results are actually being accomplished, as well as what factors are contributing or limiting these results. Without this range of information, organizational change initiatives may be inappropriately repeated or prematurely curtailed. The following suggestions and examples illustrate how these three levels of evaluation can be made to work in any organization.

Evaluating Organizational Fit

A commonly overlooked aspect of evaluation is the fit between the improvement initiative and the organization itself. This includes fit with workgroup circumstances, organization culture, business and competitive environment, leadership style, and other related factors. An assessment of fit generates learnings that increase the likelihood of successful implementation.

A Hard Look at Soft Numbers (1999 Gallop Report)

One way of assessing organizational fit is to audit factors believed to enhance or impede productivity within the organization. This usually includes components such as how people rate the quality of leadership, peoples' sense of engagement, and how people rate the meaningfulness of the work itself. Interviewing over a million employees in organizations worldwide, a Gallop organization audit found that favorable responses to 12 conditions had a consistent positive correlation with 4 business benefits — employee retention, customer retention, productivity, and profitability.[19]

The 12 Gallop workplace audit conditions:

1. I know what is expected of me at work.
2. I have the materials and equipment I need to do my work right.
3. At work, I have the opportunity to do what I do best every day.
4. In the last 7 days, I have received recognition or praise for doing good work.

5. My supervisor or someone at work seems to care about me as a person.
6. There is someone at work who encourages my development.
7. At work, my opinion seems to count.
8. The mission/purpose of my company makes me feel my job is important.
9. My associates (fellow employees) are committed to doing quality work.
10. I have a best friend at work.
11. In the last 6 months, someone at work has talked to me about my progress.
12. This last year, I have had opportunities at work to learn and grow.

Gallop surveyed based on these 12 conditions and confirmed with a significant degree of reliability that they are associated to these 4 desirable business results — employee retention, customer retention, productivity, and profitability.[20] This is a strong argument to encourage the growth of these 12 conditions in order to create an environment where these 4 business outcomes can be achieved. An assessment of these conditions, with any additional conditions unique to your workgroup or organization, might well form part of an evaluation for fit.

Another Example of an Evaluation for Fit

Fred and Merrelyn Emery's 'predictors of job satisfaction' have much in common with the Gallop study.[21] Renowned organizational theorists, the Emerys have used this tool as part of their work in participative job design. Although significant levels of job satisfaction do not always correlate strongly with superior performance, this tool nonetheless provides a useful theoretical base for assessing organizational readiness, prior to introducing an improvement initiative.

Ask each member of your workgroup to complete the following questionnaire as part of an assessment for *fit*.[22]

Compiling results from a simple, straightforward questionnaire can provide guidance on workgroup readiness. Knowing in advance what may block a needed improvement initiative equips leaders to take mitigating or corrective action and avoid predictable failure.

An Evaluation for Fit

Personal Needs

Rate the following from -5 to +5, with 0 being best (the perfect amount), +5 being far too much, and -5 being far too little.

1. Opportunities for decision-making:
- You have organizational support for making decisions in your work area.

  -5 -4 -3 -2 -1 0 +1 +2 +3 +4 +5
- You understand the goals and direction of the organization, and have the information you require for making informed decisions.

  -5 -4 -3 -2 -1 0 +1 +2 +3 +4 +5

2. Opportunities to continuously learn on the job:
- Your work is challenging and you receive timely and supportive feedback on your performance.

  -5 -4 -3 -2 -1 0 +1 +2 +3 +4 +5

3. Opportunities for variety in work:
- Your work provides ample variety.

  -5 -4 -3 -2 -1 0 +1 +2 +3 +4 +5

Work Climate

Rate the following from 0 to 10, with 10 being the best, and 0 being the worst.

4. Support and respect from co-workers:
- You are not expected to compete against your co-workers, and you can count on their support.

  0 1 2 3 4 5 6 7 8 9 10

5. Meaningful work:
- Your work has worth and quality, and provides a sense of involvement.

  0 1 2 3 4 5 6 7 8 9 10
- You know how your job fits within the whole system, and how your performance contributes to the success of the organization as a whole.

  0 1 2 3 4 5 6 7 8 9 10

6. A job that leads to a desirable future not a dead-end:
- You are able to learn, develop your skills, and grow as a person within your job.

  0 1 2 3 4 5 6 7 8 9 10

Formative Evaluation (during implementation)

Formative evaluation monitors progress during implementation, and indicates where adjustments may be needed to ensure that the initiative stays on track. It also checks to see if purported gains are being realized while the initiative is being implemented, and that there are no 'show stoppers' which could defeat the initiative before it is fully deployed. Data for formative evaluation can be collected by observation, survey, or interview, and comes from a variety of sources including service providers, clients, and co-workers.

Final Evaluation

Any confusion between *formative* and *final* evaluation can be avoided through a simple analogy. When the chef tastes the dinner while it's being prepared, that's formative evaluation. When the guests talk about the meal after they've eaten that dinner, that's final evaluation.

Final evaluation looks for the 'bottom line' impact of the improvement initiative. For example, when conducting a final evaluation on Accountability/Alignment, we work with our clients to estimate the relative cost had the identified misalignments not been resolved, and also the dollar value of new opportunities that have been implemented as part of the Accountability/Alignment process. Next, we subtract costs associated with implementing Accountability/Alignment. Our approach to final evaluation is thus:

cost savings + value of new opportunities − cost of implementing = benefits realized

Using this methodology, we find consistent results across our client organizations. For every dollar an organization spends on Accountability/ Alignment, there are significant measurable returns, in bottom line benefit, in the very first operating period. These returns can continue to be captured in the subsequent operating periods, with no further implementation costs. See sidebar for examples of misalignments identified, decisions taken, and benefits achieved using Accountability/Alignment.

Examples of Issues Resolved Using the Accountability/Alignment Process

Misalignments Identified	Decisions Taken	Benefits Achieved
• Some departments lack internal performance measures. In other cases, performance measures are not aligned across depts.	• Performance measures taken out of individual departments and assigned to one individual to set up and monitor for whole company. Clear agreement on measures across the company.	• $300k saved in staff time alone. Considerable benefits still expected from using aligned performance measures.
• No clear accountability for cash management. Company losing money on interest rate fluctuations.	• Accountability for cash management assigned, along with goals for cost reduction.	• Realistic goal set, and process in place to save $1.7m in interest costs.
• Current process for scoping-out new technologies not consistent with overall company strategy. Process results in costs without associated value for the company.	• Current process discontinued, and unnecessary costs avoided. Accountabilities assigned for monitoring new technologies, and for developing new process that is aligned with strategy.	• Estimated $1.5m cost savings. New business opportunites also anticipated, but not yet realized.
• Customer sales department just taking orders. No one is marketing and building customer relationships.	• Business case for marketing role agreed. Accountability for marketing assigned. Challenging goals set.	• 15% increase in sales from existing accounts. $387.5k in new revenue
• One department not getting the IT service that it is paying for.	• Accountability assigned. Worked with IT leader. Service issue resolved.	• IT costs reduced by 30%. A savings of $186k.
• Overlap of Business Development (BD) role, resulting in duplication of effort and unproductive competition.	• Accountability assigned by geographic region. Accountability for overall BD strategy retained by SVP.	• Minimum 10% of each department. leaders' time saved. Estimated savings of $35k.

Pre and Post Assessment

The following is an example of a questionnaire that could be distributed before introducing an organizational improvement initiative such as Accountability/Alignment, and then again following implementation of that initiative.

Workplace Assessment

(*Note whether Pre or Post an organizational improvement initiative)
Please score each item and provide a brief comment

Rating Scale: 1 = strongly disagree, 2 = disagree, 3 = agree, 4 = strongly agree

Individual

1. The business results I'm accountable for delivering are clearly defined.

1	2	3	4	Comment:

2. I can confidently exert influence within my area of accountability.

1	2	3	4	Comment:

3. I can justify saying 'no' to work I consider low value.

1	2	3	4	Comment:

Workgroup

4. Accountabilities are clear and aligned within our workgroup.

1	2	3	4	Comment:

5. People know what resources and support I require from them to be successful in my role.

1	2	3	4	Comment:

6. Our workgroup focuses its energy and time on the right business issues.

1	2	3	4	Comment:

Case Studies Demonstrating the Value of Accountability/Alignment

Case studies document a holistic approach to assessment and add another useful dimension to evaluating organizational improvement initiatives. A number of detailed case studies regarding the use of Accountability/ Alignment can be found on our website, **www.murphyklatt.com**.

Systematic Evaluation Facilitates Organizational Learning

The exclusive emphasis that many organizations place on final evaluation has resulted in a history of improvement initiatives, where, due to incomplete information, organizations are unable to repeat their successes and stop repeating their failures. Evaluating an organizational improvement initiative demands an objective and disciplined assessment of outcomes versus expectations. We recommend a systematic approach that looks at three areas of evaluation — fit, formative, and final. This provides a comprehensive picture, not just of *what* is being achieved, but also of *why* the expected benefits are or are not being realized. Data gathered in this fashion supports organizational learning and intelligent decision-making. Those improvement initiatives that add value can be repeated and improved upon, while those that do not can be modified or discarded.

Chapter 13

Avoiding Predictable Pitfalls

Aᴄᴄᴏᴜɴᴛᴀʙɪʟɪᴛʏ/Aʟɪɢɴᴍᴇɴᴛ, like any organizational improvement initiative, can self-destruct in several predictable yet avoidable ways. Here's our top ten list of nasty diversions from success. Watch for these and don't let them undermine the ongoing value you receive from this process.

Ten Nasty Diversions

1. Allowing Quality to Decline

The value received from Accountability Agreements and alignment meetings is proportional to the level of determined and creative thinking that goes into their development and maintenance. The danger is that if quality is allowed to erode, over time, the entire Accountability/Alignment approach could become inconsequential.

2. Falling off the Radar

Failing to follow through is the most common reason why improvement initiatives falter. How often have you heard comments like: "It was well implemented and working fine, but after a while it seemed to lose its place as a management priority." Recall Steven Covey's observation: "The urgent drives out the important."[23] Ongoing execution and sustainment are primarily leadership issues — military theorists call this 'maintenance of the aim.' When the leader loses faith or focus, others lose the will.

3. Losing Your Nerve

Accountability is genuine only when an individual's choices are truly his or her own. Nonetheless, a degree of uncertainty and anxiety inevitably accompanies each choice. Acting without perfect information or full control requires trust in one's judgment and courage in the face of the unknown. Wisdom lies not in denying or somehow ignoring the anxiety that accompanies accountability, but in learning how to harness the energy and anticipation that anxiety often represents. Certainly you can experience too much anxiety, and it can become paralyzing. Often however, the problem is not the anxiety itself, but how we interpret and positively manage anxiety.

It is important, for example, to recognize that unhealthy work environments do exist, and within them 'accountability' will unfortunately be a toxic term. If you work in such an environment and can't change it, you can either leave or learn to cope in some functional way. You are accountable for recognizing that you always have a choice, and for exercising the choice that is right for you and your future. The choice to leave or to adapt and stay within a given organization, like all choices, takes nerve.

4. Expecting Gain without Risk

Occasional mistakes are going to happen when people use judgment and initiative on the job. Knowing this, effective leaders need to ensure that the work environment focuses on and supports learning rather than a preoccupation with blame and punishment. Accountability Agreements require that individuals take the risk of making public commitments within the organization. For some, this can be threatening, especially those who have little confidence that promised support will be forthcoming or that mistakes will be forgiven. Taking the risk of making firm promises requires a supportive organizational environment, as well as skills in negotiation and conflict resolution.

5. Failing to Consider the Work Culture

Misalignments are surfaced as part of the Accountability/Alignment process. These then need to be dealt with openly. For example, it may be a new experience for people to publicly request a level of support from another person, or to explain why they have not achieved a promised business outcome, without fearing punishment. Developing the kind of work environment where people can talk openly about support, and the success they have and have not achieved, may indeed be a necessary leadership challenge.

Significant steps may need to be taken to prepare the organization to achieve this new way of thinking and working. Alternatively, where this support is not immediately available, Accountability/Alignment may have to be implemented incrementally and in the most receptive parts of the organization first, thereby allowing the rest of the organization to evolve as people gradually recognize the benefits being achieved from the process.

6. Unleashing an Improvement Free-For-All

Much of the competition among improvement initiatives comes from the fact that most organizations already have too many such initiatives at any one time, each scrambling for attention and scarce resources. We once asked an executive team to list all of the concurrent improvement initiatives taking place within their organization. They discovered that, in their relatively small company of 3,000 employees, there were 42 overlapping and sometimes seemingly antagonistic initiatives being implemented. Each was consuming time and money, and some were even unknown to members of the executive team. The knee-jerk reaction was to start an anti-initiative initiative. More sober thought led to culling the least productive approaches by investigating who was accountable for each of these initiatives, how they interrelated, and what results each was achieving.

7. Getting Lost in Detail

In efforts to be clear regarding accountability, as with anything else, it's always possible to go too far. Without common sense and a few safeguards, we can overshoot clarity and find ourselves lost once again. Accountability Agreements need to be kept specific, concise (just 2 or 3 pages), focused on what matters most, and kept up-to-date. This is particularly true for operational accountabilities, support requirements, and goals. Cluttering the Accountability Agreement with activities and tasks reduces clarity and dilutes the focus on end results.

8. Setting Punitive Consequences for Failure

Employees often demand more of themselves than their supervisors demand of them. They might even — in a kind of zealous heroism — invite negative consequences, which are not in their own, or the organization's best interest. We have known professionals to suggest that if they did not achieve all of their accountabilities, they should be fired. The employer's role in such circumstances is to productively redirect such fervor by emphasizing discussion and agreement on positive, not negative or punitive consequences. Further development, training, or coaching is often the first and most appropriate action where an employee has failed to achieve his or her accountabilities and goals.

9. Failing to Ensure Mutual Benefit

Above all, fairness, reasonableness, and mutuality must govern the process of Accountability/Alignment. Respect for employees as individuals with full and complex lives must be integrated with the organization's need to demand top performance from its people. All good faith business bargains are founded on the principle of a 'fair deal' within the context of a competitive marketplace economy.

10. Settling for Compliance Instead of Commitment

In 1985 Richard Walton wrote one of the most influential articles ever written on moving an organization from a culture of control to one of commitment.[24] The thrust of his article was that "workers respond best — and most creatively — not when they are tightly controlled by management, placed in narrowly defined jobs, and treated like an unwelcome necessity, but, instead, when they are given broader responsibilities, encouraged to contribute, and helped to take satisfaction in their work."[25] To ensure ongoing business success, organizations must strive for significant levels of genuine engagement. This is best accomplished by negotiating the support and resources people need to achieve their accountabilities and goals. Operating in a strictly top-down fashion renders concepts such as reciprocity, alignment, and mutual support meaningless. As discussed in Chapter 10, genuine accountability, based on vision, necessity, and design, must operate in all directions — up, down, and sideways.

It Takes Persistence

That's our top ten list of nasty diversions to avoid. They are common, but with awareness, skill, and determination, they are also entirely avoidable. Next, we move back into discussing the many ways an improvement initiative such as Accountability/Alignment can succeed. Specifically, we look at four distinct applications of Accountability/Alignment — in teams, on major projects, in the public sector, and in everyday life.

Part IV
Specific Applications

PART IV EXPLORES ACCOUNTABILITY/ALIGNMENT™ IN A RANGE OF SPECIAL APPLICATIONS.

We look at the application of Accountability/Alignment™ in work teams, on projects, and in public sector organizations. We conclude with thoughts on accountability in everyday life, including in the family, in volunteer organizations, and in education.

Chapter 14

Accountability/Alignment in Teams

THE ACCOUNTABILITY/ALIGNMENT PROCESS advanced in this book is designed specifically for today's highly skilled, interdependent, and often team-based workplace. It helps to articulate and resolve the inherent tensions between individual contribution and team expectations.

In this chapter we examine what constitutes a bona fide team, how teams are distinct from workgroups,[26] why organizations are moving toward more workgroup and team-based structures, and how clearly defined and aligned accountabilities are an essential ingredient of both workgroup and team success.

Teams are Distinct from Workgroups

The popularity of workgroups and teams today reflects the changing nature of work, which has become increasingly knowledge-based, complex, and interdependent. In many organizations, specialists combine expertise to define and solve problems that could not be addressed by any one of them alone. Indeed, the full complexity of these problems can rarely be completely understood in terms of their technical detail by other levels of management.

Teams

Through the team leader, teams are accountable for a specific product or service that is unique to the team (i.e., a whole job). Teams are units of performance, not just a type of structure or a set of values. They can't be created by edict and seldom evolve naturally in organizations. They have to be designed, developed, nurtured, and led. In addition, real teams contain a strong emotional element in their DNA that is not necessary in workgroups. That is, team members must belief in the importance of working as a team, and commit to succeeding or failing together. This is no small order. Teams work from the perspective of having a shared fate. Where this perspective is not genuine or where efforts are not made to design and develop the team, the default structure is usually the workgroup.

Workgroups

Workgroups, in contrast to teams, achieve a shared purpose by pooling individual work products. Members consult with each other and may even make some decisions together. However, most work is then delegated to and performed by individual members of the group. While a degree of interdependence is a defining feature of organizations today, members of workgroups succeed or fail as individuals, not as a team.

Individual Work

For purposes of comparison, a third type of work — that of the individual — involves a person making decisions and working almost entirely on his or her own with very little, if any, involvement with others. This level of autonomy rarely exists in modern organizations since knowledge work usually entails some level of collaboration, shared expertise, and mutual support.

Most Workgroups are Not Teams, and Don't Need to Be

'Team talk' is so fashionable today that an organization that is not team-based is often considered archaic. In practice, however, true teams — in accord with what we have outlined here — are the exception. Workgroups do not become teams just because management calls them teams, or sends them to teambuilding seminars, or even when the members of a workgroup adopt the term and refer to themselves as a team. As one person said when the team concept was inappropriately forced on his group: "It's called a team, but feels like a chain gang."

It must be emphasized that teams are not necessarily more productive than are workgroups, nor do they necessarily exercise greater influence or leverage within organizations. Structural factors determine the best way to organize (i.e., workgroup or team). These include the degree of interdependence required by the nature of the tasks that need to be accomplished, and how rewards for success are distributed.

Teamwork Behaviors

Teamwork behaviors are needed in organizations regardless of whether people structurally accomplish their work as a *team* or as a *workgroup*. Teamwork is about behaviors such as sharing information, providing mutual support, appreciating and recognizing each other's accomplishments, challenging each other's ideas in ways that build effective working relationships, and so on. Teamwork behaviors and the values that support them are an essential foundation for enabling both teams and workgroups to achieve business results.

Most Teams Fall Short of Their Potential

Companies organize people into team structures to increase productivity and improve results. And indeed, there are many examples of teams having produced outstanding business results. A more common experience, however, is that teams fail to achieve the synergies and high levels of performance expected of them.

The core issue is that teams, and the managers that appoint them, have often failed to achieve clear alignment on team member accountabilities, goals, and mutual support requirements. As a result, limiting and dysfunctional assumptions emerge leading to confusion and less than stellar business results. On the other hand, when individual team members know they are solely accountable for a specific business result, boundaries are clarified, and each is given a license to take action using his or her best business judgment within these boundaries.

When team members are not clearly aligned around their accountabilities and goals, two tendencies assert themselves. First, an individual might hold back and wait to see *who* should take action. As a result, nothing much happens and time is lost. Second, an individual, seeing that no one else is taking action, may decide to act alone. The team might not support that person's decision to act, regardless of results achieved. Either of these tendencies — doing nothing, or taking action as if the accountability were one's own — can cause teams to fragment into misunderstanding and conflict. Aligning the team leader's and each team member's individual accountabilities, at the outset, is fundamental to long-term team effectiveness and business success.

Accountabilities are Never Shared, Not Even on a Team

With teams, as with all other ways of organizing, individual accountability is the bedrock of the business relationship. And even in the best of teams, accountabilities — written promises to be personally accountable for delivering specific business results — are unique to each individual team member. As previously emphasized, it is essential to avoid writing joint, mutual, or shared accountabilities since doing so results in dubious and watered-down accountability, confused expectations, and an inability to know who has promised to be accountable for delivering what specific business result.

On occasion, a team member will balk at this idea, claiming: "Our accountabilities are too intertwined to be assigned to individual members." Such statements demonstrate confusion between the interdependent nature of team functioning and the individual nature of accountability. As a member of a team, we each own our part, and we all own the whole.

The Team Leader's Accountability Agreement Encompasses the Team's Promise of Business Results

Where there is a formal team leader, his or her individual Accountability Agreement will articulate the business results that the team, as a whole, is promising to deliver. The team leader assigns some of his or her accountabilities to individual team members. This is consistent with the operating principle that accountabilities are never shared at the same level in an organization. It also supports the notion that while a leader assigns part of his or her accountability to others, the leader also retains full accountability for the end results.

Chapter 15

Accountability/Alignment on Major Projects

W E HAVE USED ACCOUNTABILITY/ALIGNMENT with a number of large-scale, multi-year projects to assist in reducing uncertainty and creating a results-focused project culture. Our process starts with clarifying key individual accountabilities, enabling teamwork at the top, and creating sustained alignment across the project management team.

The Challenging Context of Projects

All projects are unique, temporary organizations, in that they have a defined beginning and end, and are subject to pre-established resource limits in terms of money, time, and people. This makes projects distinct from the ongoing and permanent nature of operating departments. Supplying heating oil to homes across a country is a regular operating process; building a custom oil refinery is a project. Often complex in terms of technology and management requirements, projects involve high stakes for the organizations concerned, and can rarely be done a second time if they fail the first time.

On major projects, key commitments often have to be made early, as expensive, long-lead components need to be built, often at distant locations. These early decisions lock the project into a design, which risks becoming sub-optimal if new technologies later emerge during the life of the project. A further complication arises when a completed project must be smoothly integrated into an existing operation. This final changeover — from an urgent project culture to a sustained operating culture — demands planning and an effective transition process.

Multi-Company Joint Venture Projects Can Be Even More Challenging

As complex as it may be to run a project within an established company, the difficulties become exponentially greater when several companies are involved, either as co-owners or as contractors to the owner company. The majority owner usually chooses the project manager. He or she then usually reports to a steering committee made up of executives from the various participating companies. The project manager begins by selecting a Project Management Team (PMT) from a list of individuals made available, or at least endorsed, by the participating companies.

Staffing on multi-company projects is entirely different from single company projects. Key members may have different leadership styles, cultural perspectives, allegiances, and even different business drivers. For example, contracting companies have the business pressure of maximizing their billable hours, whereas the owner company wants to contain costs. This can become particularly sensitive when contractors are given a lot of influence over major project decisions. All this means that joint venture projects are not 'business as usual,' and need to be managed differently from single company projects and ongoing strategic alliances.

Breakdowns in multi-company projects are almost always due to either the PMT's failure to clarify and maintain each party's obligations, interests, rewards, and penalties, or a steering committee's inability to define and model collaborative behavior and provide adequate project oversight. A key challenge is to provide processes which encourage each owner-organization to move beyond an exclusive focus on short-term self-interests, to more comprehensive, long-term perspectives on overall project success. The reward for project owners is having the project completed safely, on schedule, within budget, and with the required level of quality. The reward for contractors is developing long-term relationships with their client organizations, which later provide ongoing, challenging, and profitable business.

The Essential Foundation of Project Culture

Big or small, every project has a culture — defined as, 'the way we do things around here.' If not by design, then project culture exists by default. There may be little that project managers can do to protect against untimely changes in technology, the cost of capital, or changes in government policy that can affect the project. However, they can have substantial influence over the critical factors that influence how people work together.

We recommend designing project culture with the same level of care that goes into designing other aspects of the project (e.g., the project contract, project technology). There are several components essential to building an effective project culture:

1. Start with the project contract and consider how it drives behavior. People working on a project should have a shared understanding of the business proposition and drivers implicit in the contract (for example, the degree of alignment required for project success).

2. Accountabilities should be documented for each individual leader who is involved in the project. Ideally, these accountabilities are assigned to each individual based on the terms of the project contract itself, resulting in clear ownership by individuals of all aspects of the project contract.

3. In addition to setting challenging but realistic project goals, create a unique project identity including a project logo, mission statement, and operating principles. This can give people something to be proud of and around which they can unite their efforts — a way of distinguishing themselves that is separate from their home companies.

4. Give people the necessary organizational tools. For example:

- Teach people how to hold efficient meetings so this time is spent productively.
- Teach people how to raise and constructively resolve conflicts so that differences don't get buried until it's too late to take effective action.
- Make sure people are speaking the same project language. (See sidebar below for an example of misunderstood terminology.)
- Provide the necessary information technology support and ensure that people can use the selected software to get the job done. We have seen a great deal of time wasted due to lack of familiarity with designated project management systems.

5. Jointly create a set of leadership and behavioral norms for the project. Insist on their application. Make these public, and frequently measure success against these norms. Review this regularly at PMT meetings.

6. Hold teambuilding events so that everyone understands each other's perspective, and has the opportunity to enjoy their working time together.

7. Stay aligned. Use the Accountability/Alignment process to ensure that original intentions are retained. Resolve gaps and overlaps, and defuse misunderstandings. Discuss progress, performance, and ongoing support requirements at regular workgroup meetings.

8. Build a project performance management system with Accountability Agreements as part of its foundation to track success in achieving accountabilities and goals across the entire project. One small example serves to illustrate. A major project that we consulted to took the courageous step of posting its task and team performance feedback by the elevator door in the building where they operated. Anyone interested could see how

the project was doing on important performance and cultural indicators.

9. Communicate and celebrate. Use newsletters, email, and town hall meetings so that people know about important events on the project. Celebrate milestones. Include everyone or as many people as possible. Use mementos and project souvenirs so people feel and know that they belong, that they matter, that their efforts count, and that they are part of a successful project.

The most serious and visible difficulties on joint venture projects arise when Steering Committees or PMTs fail to align around accountabilities or goals, or around issues of culture and leadership. This is occasionally a consequence of leaders being given inconsistent marching orders by their parent companies, or working from conflicting and even hidden agendas. Such failures are most often due to faulty and untested assumptions and poorly defined expectations.

In addition to the visible costs of cultural misalignment, there is the issue of 'invisible waste.' Over the last decade, project organizations have made great strides in eliminating visible waste by using state of the art estimating, expediting, and procurement systems. But invisible waste occurs when people don't understand what they and others are accountable for, when work falls into gaps that no one owns, when people are protecting individual turf, or when people are looking after the interests of their parent organization to the detriment of the overall project. Problems of cultural misalignment and 'invisible waste' are best addressed early in a project, and are easier to avoid than they are to repair.

Better Tools are Needed for Project Culture Building and Alignment

Many project managers know the 'cost and opportunity curve'. The opportunity to make a significant impact on the overall cost and quality is greatest early in the project. Once the design is set and major commitments are made, however, there is less flexibility. Ideas that could have saved money at the beginning become less relevant later. For example, once you have hired a contracting company it might not matter that you could achieve considerable savings by using a particular type of project management software, if the contracting company cannot support this particular application.

This is also true of leadership and cultural issues where work styles and patterns of relating become firmly established. It is difficult to correct dysfunctional behavioral norms, such as tardiness or non-cooperation, after they have become habitual on a project. An early and fully informed discussion provides the best opportunity to create and model a project culture, based on the operating principles underlying Accountability/ Alignment (these operating principles are discussed in Chapters 2 and 3).

The inescapable and potentially costly issue of rework is also represented on this 'cost and opportunity curve.' On large, complex projects, the focus is always on how to minimize rework, keep costs down, and stay on schedule. The usual rule of thumb for such situations is this: for every development phase where a piece of rework passes through undetected, costs increase exponentially (Boehm, 1981).[27] Alan Graham makes this point dramatically. Using a factor of 10 for rework, he says: "That's one hour in the specification phase, 10 hours in design, 100 hours in implementation, and 1,000 hours in system test phase."[28] A PMT that regularly reviews project progress from a foundation of aligned and clearly articulated individual accountabilities will emphasize catching and resolving problems early, before rework costs take their toll on the budget.

Implementing and Sustaining Accountability/ Alignment on a Project

Project leaders need a process to monitor and manage both individual and project level performance throughout the life of the project. The process starts with individual accountability that is clear, complete, and accepted for each of the roles identified in the project contract.

We know of one multi-billion dollar project, for example, that ran into serious schedule and budget problems due to a simple lack of alignment.

Project Improvement using Accountability/Alignment

Alignment Process Surfaces Fundamental Misunderstanding

An engineering contractor working with an energy company didn't realize that their 'project management terminology' was getting them into trouble. Each party was using the same terminologies, but to convey a very different meaning. Terms such as 'design basis memorandum' and 'stage gate process' were used by both parties, but with very different interpretations. What made this problem dangerous was that neither party realized they were not talking the same language. This issue was surfaced at the PMT alignment meeting. Raising this single issue clarified critical meanings, saved thousands of dollars, and avoided days of fruitless effort that would otherwise have been expended by the engineering team.

Technical Leader Joins Well After Project Start Up

Half way through the engineering design phase of a project, a new leader was assigned to a sub project — designing and building a co-generation plant. On his first day on the project, the new leader, along with the project's senior engineer, worked with us to write the new leader's Accountability Agreement. Later that day, the new leader reviewed his Accountability Agreement with his boss. The new leader was now up to speed and clear on his role, goals, and schedule, right from the beginning of his assignment.

Project Manager uses Accountability/Alignment to Manage Performance

Prior to implementing Accountability/Alignment, the EPC contractor, who was also the Project Manager, explained what success would look like — very specific accountabilities and clearly defined goals. He wanted to know exactly who was accountable for what and by when on the project. He used Accountability Agreements to manage performance. He met with his direct reports as a group every two weeks. During these meetings he used Accountability Agreements to track each direct report's progress on his or her accountabilities and goals, and to ensure each was receiving the support required from others to be successful.

Client and Project Management Groups Achieve Alignment

Accountability Agreements were completed for each member of the project management team, both on the client side and contractor side. An alignment meeting then followed. This was the first time the client project management group and the contract project management group had met as one team. Numerous alignment issues were discussed and resolved, including the actual studies the client expected the contractor to complete, the level of detail the client expected during the design phase of the project, the lead indicators for cost and schedule issue identification, and the process to be used to make key project decisions, such as deciding on the project expansion footprint.

Achieving a Turnaround in a Large Systems Project

An information systems project, with an estimated cost between $195 and $210 million, had been drifting for a year without producing results. We started by clarifying and aligning Accountability Agreements within the PMT — including resetting goals and agreeing on mutual support requirements. Very quickly, people started to notice improvement. The next level of project leadership then articulated and aligned their Accountability Agreements, resulting in vastly improved clarity around cost, schedule, and quality, as well as significant improvement in overall project alignment and morale. A year later the project was completed and declared a significant business success.

It started with the appointment of several senior managers — all called 'project managers.' A number of these individuals refused to accept any limitations on their role based on the needs of the other 'project managers.' People were also working with several versions of the project schedule, and new versions — sometimes unauthorized — were regularly produced. Sadly, this project involved several hundred well-intentioned yet confused participants, and saw tens of millions of dollars wasted, all due to a lack of fundamental alignment of roles and accountabilities. This could have been overcome with the proper implementation of a process such as Accountability/Alignment.

Creating a Productive Project Organization

In a project world full of surprises, missed opportunities, and disappointments, the people who are focused are most likely to succeed. Many sophisticated project management tools have been developed over the years to assist with the technical elements of project success. Accountability/Alignment has been created to manage the critical culture and people components.

Chapter 16

Accountability/Alignment in Public Service

WE ARE HEARTENED TO SEE A NUMBER OF AMBITIOUS UNDERTAKINGS in the public service sector, in both Canada and the United States, that align with our insights on accountability. Two significant examples are the Canadian Treasury Board's[29] support for accountability within the framework of results-based management, and the U.S. General Accounting Office use of performance agreements.[30]

Understanding accountability in the public service requires making an initial distinction between political accountability and administrative accountability. Politicians set policy and priorities, and determine how public money will be spent. Their performance in democratic societies is evaluated with some finality at election time. Citizen satisfaction with the keeping of political promises, and the degree of alignment with the electorate, determines a politician's tenure.

Public administrators, on the other hand, are charged with ensuring that the 'will of government' is carried out, so that citizens receive legislated programs and services. To this end, the public service manages and delivers programs, and is accountable for all that transpires under the umbrella of their administrative portfolio. It is accountability in the public service, at the program management and administrative level, not at the political level, that is the focus of this chapter.

Defining Accountability in the Public Service

At the administrative level, public service management of programs is not substantially different from that in the private sector. Room for accountability within the public service exists once the political agenda is decided, budget allocations made, and priorities set. Measurable results can be assessed with reference to the stated objectives of the programs that have been mandated by the political party in power.

As straightforward as the notion of public sector accountability may be in theory, achieving it is no small undertaking. One of the first roadblocks is a clear understanding of what it means to be 'accountable' in the public sector. A report by the Canadian Treasury Board in 2002 begins the discussion of accountability with the following paragraph:

Conventional media interpretation and ordinary discourse often inter-pret accountability simply as a process of assigning blame and punishing wrongdoing. In contrast, modern governance and public administration literature, and in some cases practice, sees accountability more as a positive incentive — as an opportunity to demonstrate achievements and stewardship. In this view, accountability is an integral and indispensable part of establishing effective relationships for getting things done and taking responsibility, including assigning authority and resources.[31]

The report highlights the significant change in thinking that is taking place about accountability in the public service. It first quotes a traditional definition of accountability as follows: "Accountability is the obligation to answer for a responsibility conferred." The writer of the report notes that such a definition implies a servile mentality — an uncritical following of orders. A more useful definition is then offered: "Accountability is a relationship based on the obligation to demonstrate and take responsibility for performance in light of agreed expectations." This second perspective clearly underscores the obligation to answer for what has been accomplished or not accomplished. It captures the essence of accountability in knowledge-based work environments, where working relationships and the need to influence predominate, and where formal authority alone is rarely sufficient to achieve meaningful results.

The Treasury Board report goes on to note:

A focus on performance covers the benefits accomplished for citizens, as well as due process and fairness in the delivery of services. In demonstrating performance against agreed expectations, the need to balance greater flexibility and autonomy with enhanced accountability for results, and the need for openness and transparency is made evident. The 'agreement' (regarding expectations) referred to is either an explicit or implicit agreement between subordinates and superiors in a hierarchical relationship, or the agreement between partners in a less hierarchical relationship.[32]

Such a reinterpretation of accountability makes it possible to imagine a more responsive, entrepreneurial public service where people are focused on outcomes for citizens as well as on improvements of internal processes. The agreement regarding expectations seems to be founded on the concept of a basic bargain, or what we call the 'fair deal' between an employee and his or her employer.

Another aspect of accountability is the issue of control versus influence. The author of the Treasury Board report leaves no doubt about the stand taken by the Board:

> Accountability for results asks if you have done everything possible with your authorities and resources towards affecting the achievement of intended results, and if you have learned from past experience what works and doesn't work. Accounting for results of this kind means demonstrating that you have made a difference; that through your actions and efforts you have contributed to the results achieved. It means you are accountable for what you can influence, as well as what you can directly control.[33]

The author of the Treasury Board report goes on to discuss management flexibility — the necessary 'elbow room' needed by each public service leader to exercise and be accountable for a level of individual judgment and decision-making:

> And the greater management flexibility, which has often accompanied a greater focus on results, provides the needed means to better manage your ability to influence outcomes. Demonstrating the results you have achieved, including what you have influenced, provides the evidence of effective stewardship of the greater flexibilities made available.[34]

Encouraging Examples of Early Success

It appears that the main obstacle to a full understanding and implementation of accountability in government is that convention and precedent are given so much authority. A great deal of effort is being expended to constructively challenge current convention and some encouraging examples are creating new precedents.

One of the most practical examples comes from the U.S. General Accounting Office (GAO) whose tag line is: 'Accountability – Integrity – Reliability.'[35] The U.S. federal government has been experimenting with 'performance agreements' since 1993. These agreements have been established with senior executives in a number of agencies (Department of Transportation, Veterans Health Administration, the Office of Student Financial Assistance), and are very explicit regarding outcomes to be achieved, and positive consequences to be awarded for success.

This approach has proceeded to the extent that in 1998 Congress chartered several government organizations as Performance Based Organizations (PBOs), insisting that they implement performance agreements as a normal part of their management process. The GAO report of October 2000 states: "Under the PBO legislation, progress towards the goals in performance agreements is to serve as the basis by which to determine the amount of any annual performance bonuses for the Chief Operating Officer and the senior managers."[36] This GAO report also noted that a number of agencies are implementing the 'performance agreement' approach throughout their organizations.

The GAO noted 5 key benefits derived from their experiments with outcomes-based performance. They found that performance agreements:[37]

1. strengthened alignment of results-oriented goals with daily operations
2. fostered collaboration across organizational boundaries
3. enhanced opportunities to discuss and routinely use performance information to make program improvements
4. provided a results-oriented basis for individual accountability

5. provided a way to maintain continuity of program goals during leadership transitions

Current government initiatives to create accountability emphasize connecting goals to strategy, and the necessary relationship between results and rewards. Notwithstanding these efforts in Canada and the U.S., as well as other countries such as Britain, Australia, and New Zealand, the task of focusing government organizations on results, instead of on internal processes and procedures, still faces some major obstacles. These include an appreciation of the importance of mutual support and alignment across workgroups, and the need to facilitate inter-agency and inter-department work.

If It's a Trap, It Won't Work

The actions of political leaders can be a support or impediment to an outcomes-based approach in the public sector. If the notion of accountability is used to facilitate political buck passing and blaming, it will die a quick death. In this way, accountability would be seen as a trap — easy to set, and easy to avoid. Much of the goal-setting process known as MBO (Management by Objectives) was of this nature. The art was in the ability to write objectives that sounded challenging, but were nonetheless defensible when not fulfilled. Much creative literary energy was spent on this task.

There is always the temptation in the political arena for opposition parties to use 'outcomes-based performance plans' as a way to embarrass the government. Knowing that an agency has committed to certain outcomes, it is possible to stymie their efforts, and, in doing so, humble the governing party. In this way, the honest effort to be more accountable could backfire and become a cynical political game.

One solution is for public service executives to get agreement on clearly articulated support requirements with their political leaders, and to make their individual Accountability Agreements, including these statements of support, a matter of public record. This would take a degree of cultural change at the political level, but would be well worth the effort.

The Need for Cultural Change in the Public Sector

Culture change is another challenge for government agencies. The GAO refers to the necessity for a 'cultural transformation' in how government operates, and the Canadian Treasury Board report is sobering in this regard. It cautions agencies to be prepared to take a number of years to implement the shift from focusing on activities to focusing on results. Our experience regarding time requirements is more optimistic, but we agree with the principle stated by the Treasury Board — that it is best to begin with pilot projects where the benefits can be clearly demonstrated, and then apply this work more broadly to other divisions or departments in the public service.

Cultural change is facilitated through education on the operating principles of accountability and alignment, followed by an uncomplicated and measurable implementation approach. When people see successful examples on the part of 'early adopters,' they are then inspired to use Accountability Agreements for themselves and with members of their work teams.

Current government initiatives to create a culture of accountability emphasize connecting goals to strategy, and the necessary relationship between results achieved and rewards. Yet, as encouraging as these initiatives are, they fall short in the following key areas:

- recognition of the unique experience of each knowledge worker
- appreciation of the leadership values of each knowledge worker
- the need to improve mutual support and alignment across workgroups
- the need to facilitate interagency and inter-department work
- the need to consider the entire job, not just a few high profile accountabilities

Anyone attempting to improve the culture in their part of a public sector organization will find the following discussion of these key areas helpful.

Recognition of the Unique Experience and Perception of Each Knowledge Worker

The need for each individual to craft his or her role to suit distinctive perspectives and talents is not emphasized in current government practice. Every leader is hired to contribute his or her unique gifts to the job, and to put a somewhat different flavor on the department or agency as a result. Accountability/Alignment captures this in the business focus statement of each individual's Accountability Agreement·

The business focus statement outlines the individual's unique value proposition. It provides an opportunity to articulate the individual's perception of his or her role, and to have this supported by his or her immediate supervisor. This can preclude enormous frustration and misunderstanding, since it is no longer a surprise when an individual takes strong stands on some issues, while downplaying others.

Appreciation of the Leadership Values of Each Knowledge Worker

Leadership accountabilities focus on means. They provide others in the organization with a clear understanding of the cultural and leadership values held by the accountable individual. The following example illustrates this point: an agency group had a history of making agreements but then not following through. Their leader created a new leadership accountability for himself: 'Ensuring that action is taken quickly where commitments are not being met.' From then on, no commitment was allowed to expire unchallenged. Soon people began to make promises more carefully and follow-through became the norm.

Documenting only 'ends' leaves the 'means' to those ends silent. People want to know what their manager values in terms of behavior, style, and culture. Reading what a person declares as his or her leadership accountabilities expedites understanding and effective working relationships. In this way, people know what they can expect and what will be expected of them.

The Need to Improve Mutual Support and Alignment Across Workgroups

Conspicuously absent from government practice of accountability are the critical elements of mutual support and cross-functional alignment.

Working at cross-purposes is all too common in large bureaucracies, and people are frustrated where their initiative is met with resistance or unresponsiveness. It is not enough for an individual to be clear on his or her accountabilities and goals; others in the organization also have to be aligned in terms of the goals they too are working to achieve. Aligning people's interest with that of the department or agency, and among all organizational members, is the key to sustained success.

To this end, a significant step forward for government employees will be to articulate the interactive nature of the work itself. Nobody gets their job done without the assistance of many others in knowledge-based work environments. The ability to declare a need for support, and then to articulate and negotiate this with key individuals, could by itself positively transform many government-employee relationships among peers, managers, and political leaders.

The Need to Facilitate an Increasing Amount of Interagency and Interdepartmental Work

There has been considerable growth in interdepartmental, intergovernmental, and interagency work within government. Increasingly, projects are sharing funding from more than one department, or from public, private, and not-for-profit sectors. As a result, government agencies need better processes to consistently and reliably achieve clarity concerning mutual support requirements among interdependent agencies and departments. A tool such as Accountability/Alignment is needed to clarify the obligations of each participant on projects that cut across departmental boundaries. Accountability/Alignment clarifies exactly who owns what result, and what level and type of support is required to achieve project success.

By way of example, two government departments that had worked at cross-purposes in the past realized they could accomplish more by working together than by working alone, or by competing. The senior leaders from each department were invited to attend the other department's alignment meeting. This improved understanding considerably, and set a new and lasting tone of mutual support and collaboration.

Incorporating Balanced Scorecard with Accountability/Alignment

Balanced scorecard measures are easily gathered and organized once Accountability Agreements are complete and aligned. By the same token, where balanced scorecard measures are already in place, these can be used as a check to ensure Accountability Agreements are complete. Whichever process is used first, there needs to be consistency among accountabilities, goals, and balanced scorecard measures.

You might want to include key leadership accountabilities on the balanced scorecard. These are the behaviors and the work culture required to achieve the operational accountabilities and goals. Post and continually update progress toward balanced scorecard measures, and who is accountable for each, in a visible place within the organization (e.g., intranet, wall charts). Each balanced scorecard measure should be assigned to one and only one person, even though several others will have support roles in helping the accountable individual to achieve these measures. This is the operating principle of single point accountability.

The Need to Consider the Entire Job, Not Just a Few High Profile Accountabilities

There remains a tendency in government to apply the operating principles of accountability to only the higher profile projects (e.g., those that secure separate funding from central agencies). Yet, as has been seen in Canada in the case of the HRDC[38] debacle, it is rarely the high profile initiatives that lead to the perception of mismanagement. Rather, this perception takes place when there is a lack of clarity about who is accountable for simply following the more mundane but essential standard practices.

Accountability/Alignment provides the flexibility to capture both the high profile goals that need to be measured in the current period, and all relevant yet material accountabilities that must be met year after year in government roles. The rigor of Accountability/Alignment ensures that there is no doubt about who is accountable for following approved practices. In this way, public sector leaders can count on their people being clear about their individual accountabilities and goals, in support of ongoing prudence and transparency in government practice.

Accountability/Alignment Moves Intention to Action

Our public organizations reflect our limitless aspirations — exercised with limited funds. The public today expects more accountability from public institutions, is more vigilant regarding waste and corruption, and more organized to pressure governments to achieve meaningful results. Information technology has driven greater transparency and makes it increasingly possible for citizens to monitor and influence the performance of public organizations. As pressure for transparency and results continues, government agencies will become more determined and capable of continuously improving their organizational effectiveness.

Chapter 17

Accountability/Alignment in Everyday Life

A MOVEMENT TO CLEARER ACCOUNTABILITY WILL BE LED by the growing legion of knowledge workers, the most skilled of which will always be in short supply. These highly skilled workers will enjoy an influential lifestyle and degree of independence to which others will aspire. And because of the great demand for their talent, most will be able to demand challenging and interesting work. Many will work as free agents on a contractual basis using a framework such as an Accountability Agreement to document their reciprocal business bargains with their employers.

On an even larger scale, business and industry generally will be more responsive to stakeholders, and will be increasingly transparent in terms of how they make decisions and operate. Executives will compete to demonstrate the transparency of their processes and decisions to investors, customers, and employees alike. The age-old game of 'buck passing' will be checked, and whistle blowers will receive public service awards.

The changes we envision will affect each of us on a personal, family, community, and organizational level. Our hope is that we eventually find ourselves living in a more creative, productive, and 'no excuses' culture.

Accountability in the Family

People participating in our Accountability/Alignment process frequently take these ideas home for family conversations. Given an objective approach to emotional topics, they often have moving conversations

Building Your Reputation as an Accountable Individual

A person's reputation is his or her stock-in-trade. It enhances the ability to influence and greatly contributes to organizational and social success. Michael Angier offers these suggestions for building one's reputation as an accountable individual.[39]

- Take all agreements seriously — keep all promises, even minor ones.
- Be careful what you agree to — don't give your word lightly.
- Keep track of your agreements — organize your commitments, write them down, check them off.
- Make sure your agreements are clear — send an email to ensure understanding, resolve differences promptly.
- Be careful with whom you make agreements — avoid or document agreements with people who tend to break them.
- Renegotiate immediately when you are not able to keep your agreements — even if this makes you uncomfortable.
- Manage by agreement — dialogue regularly to ensure understanding and agreement.

Every Promise You Make Matters to Someone

When you let someone down, when you fail to keep a promise, when you don't show up for a meeting on time, when you tell someone that you will call them next week but don't, or when you miss your child's concert even though you promised to be there, it's important to stop and notice your level of consciousness about your promises. You may have something to learn about yourself. Usually others don't care about 'why' you let them down. What they do wonder about is how reliable your next promise is likely to be.

about what they can fairly expect of each other in the family. In this way, they 'check in' with each other to ensure that their expectations are reasonable, and that other family members are willing to work to fulfill agreed expectations.

High School Student Seeking a Summer Job

A leader who became familiar with Accountability/Alignment while working with us on a project related an interesting example. He took his Accountability Agreement home and shared it with his family. His son, a high school student who was looking for a summer job, decided to use the Accountability Agreement format to apply for a much-sought-after job at a local factory. Two days after he sent in his Accountability Agreement, he got an interview from the factory's Human Resources manager who immediately offered him a job, saying: "You're hired. I've never met a seventeen year old who wanted to be accountable for anything."

Some of the greatest family benefits come from discussions of mutual support, and from being specific about what help and encouragement each family member needs from others. A frank discussion of the natural consequences of behavior as a family member can be enlightening, even transforming. Similar to organizational work, the application of a prescribed process can make it possible to have constructive conversations instead of intractable conflicts.

This is not to say that family relationships should or will become simply transactional, or that the consequences of Accountability/Alignment in the family context are simply the equivalent of business results. However, there are some transactional aspects to family functioning (e.g., you can borrow the car if you mow the lawn). Such aspects can easily be put into a constructive and mutually supportive framework for creating clear agreements and aligned expectations. This, in turn, can help to improve family functioning, increase harmony, and teach accountability to children and adults alike.

Accountability in Nonprofit and Volunteer Organizations

Nonprofits exist to provide a service to their stakeholders instead of shareholders. While nonprofits are always interested in fundraising and might generate profits in any given year, profitability is not their intended purpose. Yet accountability is as necessary in any not-for-profit organization as it is in a private-for-profit or public sector organization. The CEO on a nonprofit, reporting to the Board of Directors, is personally accountability for everything the organization does or fails to do. The Board in turn is accountable to the stakeholders, and indeed to the public, since it is their goodwill that makes charitable donations available.

In view of a few very high-profile scandals, many nonprofits today face significant accountability pressures. Accordingly, nonprofits are being asked to justify and make clear their management fees, levels of performance, responsiveness to clients, ethics, and use of funds. As a result, many nonprofits are actively incorporating processes and measures that demonstrate accountability to their stakeholders (e.g., clients, foundations, government donors, the public at large.)

As accountability becomes a more pervasive value in society, volunteer organizations may be among the many beneficiaries of this new attitude. These organizations are similar to families, in that purpose and relationships are central, and the profit motive is not driving behavior. At the same time, clear, agreed, and reciprocal expectations are critical to the ability of volunteer organizations to attract, retain, and guide the efforts of skilled volunteers.

John Carver, perhaps the foremost authority on the design of governing Boards of Directors in non-profit organizations, challenges what he calls the 'red herring' of volunteerism.[40] This is the often untested and unspoken assumption that because people are volunteers, they should not be held to the same standards of performance as are paid employees.

We have found that explicit Accountability Agreements, where people clarify their promises and live up to each other's expectations, add tremendous value to the alignment of effort in volunteer organizations. In these organizations, accountability often focuses on areas such as commitment to timelines, contribution at meetings, and achieving fund raising targets, but can be extended to behavioral issues as part of the leadership accountabilities section of the Accountability Agreement. These include notions such as respectful dialogue and seeking solutions instead of blaming.

Accountabilities of Parents, Players, and Coaches in a Children's Baseball League

The following example shows how accountability statements can be used to outline standards and ensure clarity and commitment to appropriate roles and practices within a children's sports association. This agreement was discussed with each official, parent, and child within this children's baseball league.

Parent's Accountabilities

I am personally accountable for:

a) supporting my child's choice to play baseball (this is his or her choice, not mine)

b) my child playing by the rules and resolving conflict without violence

c) my child understanding that doing his or her best is as important as winning

d) helping my child to enjoy the game through praise for fair play and good effort

e) not ridiculing or yelling at my child for making a mistake or losing a game

f) applauding good effort on either team (children learn best from example)

g) not questioning a league official's judgment or honesty in public

h) respecting and showing appreciation for the volunteer umpires and coaches

i) supporting all efforts to remove verbal and physical abuse from ball games

Player's Accountabilities

I am personally accountable for:

a) playing baseball because I want to, not because other people want me to play

b) playing by the rules of the game and within the spirit of the game

c) respecting my opponents and controlling my temper (mouthing-off spoils the game)

d) being a team player and supporting the team, and not just my own individual success

e) having fun, making friends, doing my best, improving my skills (winning isn't everything)

f) respecting and appreciating umpires and coaches (they are there to help me)

Coach's Accountabilities

I am personally accountable for:

a) scheduling practices and games while respecting players' other obligations

b) teaching my players to play fairly, respect rules, umpires, and opponents

c) all players getting an equitable amount of instruction, support, and playing time

d) setting a good example of leadership (being generous in my praise, encouraging players to have confidence in themselves, not ridiculing or yelling at players for making mistakes or performing badly)

e) equipment and facilities being safe and suitable for player ages and abilities

f) continuing to develop my own abilities as a coach (e.g., attending coaching seminars, knowing the rules, maintaining good relationships with league officials)

g) working cooperatively with officials for the betterment of the league and the game

Accountability in Education

Public schooling is one of the largest, most complex, and most expensive collective functions in society. Our hope is that schools will adopt Accountability/Alignment and evolve authentic notions of accountability. The practice of making and keeping promises, while supporting others, will enable those in the educational process to reach greater levels of accomplishment.

Much of the confusion and frustration regarding public schooling comes from misaligned expectations of what teachers and students are supposed to achieve together. Examples include a lack of clarity about support required from parents and school administrators, and serious misapprehensions regarding educational policy at the government level. As such, educators who are hungry for change tell us that accountability must become a core skill for schools.

At the classroom level, the disciplined framing and articulation of accountability will reduce teacher frustration by providing a positive framework for the give and take of the educational process. At the school and district level, it will make the support that the teacher is able to provide visible for discussion and negotiation, and facilitate alignment with the reciprocal obligations of students, parents, and administrators.

A Closing Note On Our Mission

Our dream is that a commitment to genuine accountability will generate a renewal of public confidence, out of the current disillusionment and cynicism regarding business and government organizations. We feel that embracing and enacting this fundamental ethic among individuals, families, communities, and corporations will increase prosperity and improve quality of life. We hope that, through this book, we have contributed a set of operating principles and useful tools that will inspire people to make necessary and ambitious promises — and then to keep them.

Part V
Appendices

Appendix 1: The Accountability/Alignment™ Process.

Appendix 2: The Accountability Agreement® Template.

Appendix 3: Key Definitions.

Appendix 4: Selected Readings.

The Accountability/Alignment™ Process

Steps

- *Accountability* – develop individual Accountability Agreements
- *Alignment* – align Accountability Agreements within and across workgroups
- *Achievement* – use the process to ensure business results

Operating Principles

Accountability

1. is personal and not shared at the same level in an organization
2. is for business results
3. requires room for personal judgment
4. is unconditional — no excuses
5. is primary for the organization as a whole and belongs to everyone
6. is founded on a fair business bargain

Alignment

1. links up individual accountabilities at the group level
2. resolves gaps and overlaps of accountabilities and goals
3. achieves agreement on mutual support
4. requires a foundation of strategy, structure, and leadership

5. is best achieved using the 80/20 rule
6. is dynamic and requires regular tune-ups

Achievement

1. Accountability/Alignment becomes the vehicle for aligning roles
2. Accountability Agreements are used regularly to organize work
3. Accountability Agreements are updated and realigned regularly
4. leaders model accountable and aligned behavior
5. the process is used to complement existing practices
6. the process is audited and continuously improved

Appendix 2

The Accountability Agreement™ Template

Accountability Agreement

Name: _____

Title: _____

Date: _____

Business Focus Statement

_____

_____

_____

_____

_____

_____

_____

Operational Accountabilities

I am personally accountable for:

a) _____

b) _____

c) _____

Leadership Accountabilities

I am personally accountable for:

a) _____

b) _____

Support Requirements

I require the following support from:

      Name: _____

a) _____

      Name: _____

a) _____

Goals

a) _____

b) _____

Sustainment Plan

a) _____

b) _____

Positive Consequences

(confidential between individual and manager)

a) _____

b) _____

Appendix 3

Key Definitions

Accountability – A personal promise and obligation to deliver business results.

Accountability Agreement® – A results-based outline of an individual's business bargain outlining his or her contribution to delivering the organization's strategy.

Accountability/Alignment™ – Individual Accountability Agreements are developed, aligned, and used to guide achievement of business results.

Alignment – The application of individual accountability at the group level.

Gap – A necessary business outcome without an owner.

Interdependency – Relationships where individuals depend on each another for a product or service

Overlap – A necessary business outcome that has more than one owner.

Appendix 4

Selected Readings

A few of our favorite books that touch on the topic of Accountability:

Bossidy, L., Charan, R. and Burck, C. (2002). *Execution: The discipline of getting things done*. New York, NY: Random House.

Gardner, J.W. (1990). *On Leadership*. New York, NY: The Free Press.

Goleman, D. (1985). *Vital lies, simple truths: The psychology of self-deception*. New York, NY: Touchstone.

Koestenbaum, P. and Block, P. (2001). *Freedom and accountability at work: Applying philosophic insight to the real world*. San Francisco, CA: Jossey-Bass/Pfeiffer.

Reich, R.B. (2001) *The future of success*. New York, NY: Alfred A. Knopf.

Sykes, C.J. (1992) *A nation of victims: The decay of the American character*. New York, NY: St. Martin's Press.

Endnotes

[1] Throughout this book we use the term 'alignment' as a short form of the term 'workforce alignment.'

[2] Reich, Robert B. (2001) *The future of success*. New York, NY: Alfred A. Knopf.

[3] Mills, D.Q. (1991) *Rebirth of the corporation*. New York, NY: John Wiley & Sons, p. 69.

[4] Covey, Stephen R. (1989) *The 7 habits of highly effective people: Powerful lessons in personal change*. New York, NY: Simon & Schuster.

[5] Bossidy, L., Charan, R. and Burck, C. (2002) *Execution: The discipline of getting things done*. New York, Ny: Random House, p. 3.

[6] Jim Kouzes is chairman emeritus of the Tom Peters Company. He is also an executive fellow at the Center for Innovation and Entrepreneurship at the Leavey School of Business, Santa Clara University, in Silicon Valley, California.

[7] Roughly summarized from: Klatt, B., S. Murphy, and D. Irvine (2003). *Accountability: Getting a grip on results* (2nd rev. ed.). Calgary, AB: Bow River Publishing.

[8] Bossidy, L., Charan, R. and Burck, C. (2002) *Execution: The discipline of getting things done*. New York, NY: Random House. p. 48–9.

[9] For a modern interpretation of Machiavelli with examples from current world events see: Ledeen, Michael, A. (1999). *Machiavelli on modern leadership: Why Machiavelli's iron rules are as timely and important today as five centuries ago*. New York, NY: Truman Talley Books.

[10] Dave Irvine, a friend and former co-author, inspired this sidebar.

[11] Sydney Harris has delighted millions with his irreverent cartoons. Just a few of his many publications include: *Can't you guys read? Cartoons on Academia* (1991), *49 dogs, 36 cats and a platypus* (1999), *The five biggest ideas in science* (1997), and *Freudian slips: Cartoons on psychology* (1997).

[12] D. Quinn Mills makes a similar argument noting that: "Responsibility is about doing something right; accountability is about doing the right thing." Mills, D.Q. (1991). *Rebirth of the corporation*. New York, NY: John Wiley & Sons, p. 43.

[13] Gray, J. (2003). *Al Qaeda and what it means to be modern*. New York, NY: The New Press, p. 42.

[14] The term 'action learning' can be traced back to Kurt Lewin's work in the 1940s. Marvin Weisbord explains that the term was intended to embrace *"enhanced problem-solving … [and to] preserve democratic values, build commitment to act, and motivate learning — all at once."* See: Weisbord, M.R. (1989). *Productive workplaces: Organizing and managing for dignity, meaning, and community*. San Francisco, CA: Jossey-Bass, p. 187.

[15] Examples of readings on organizational learning and change:
- Senge, P., Ross, R., Smith, B., Roberts, C., and Kleiner, A. (1994). *The fifth discipline fieldbook: Strategies and tools for building a learning organization*. New York, NY: Currency Doubleday.
- Jick, T.D. (1993). *Managing change: Cases and concepts*. Burr Ridge, IL: Irwin.
- Kotter, John P. (1996). *Leading change*. Boston, MA: Harvard Business School Press.
- Beers, M., Eisenstat, R.A., and Spector, B. (1990). "Why change programs don't produce change," *Harvard Business Review*, (November-December) p. 158–166.

Examples of readings on personal habit change:
- Seligman, M.E.P. (1993). *What you can change … and what you can't: The complete guide to successful self-improvement*. New York, NY: Fawcett Columbine.
- Rechtschaffen, S. (1996). *Timeshifting. Creating more time to enjoy your life*. New York, NY: Doubleday.
- Campbell, Susan M. (1995). *From chaos to confidence: Survival strategies for the new workplace*. New York, NY: Simon & Schuster.
- Covey, S.R. (1989). *The 7 habits of highly effective people: Powerful lessons in personal change*. New York, NY: Simon & Schuster.

[16] The term 'modeling the way' comes from Jim Kouzes and Barry Posner.

[17] Roughly summarized from: Klatt, B., Murphy, S., and Irvine, D. (2003) *Accountability: Getting a grip on results* (2nd rev. ed). Calgary, AB: Bow River Publishing.

[18] The notion of a 'balanced scorecard' has become popular, particularly in public sector organizations, as a way of balancing qualitative and non financial goals with the traditional 'single focus' on financial measures of success. See: Kaplan, R.S., and Norton, D.P. (1996). *The balanced scorecard: Translating strategy into action*. Boston, MA: Harvard Business School Press.

[19] Coffman, C., and Harter, J., (March 1999), *A hard look at soft numbers: The relationship between employee perceptions and business outcomes*. The Gallop Organization. <http://gmj.gallup.com>

[20] Gallop reviewed these 12 conditions for content validity (the degree to which these 12 conditions align with good theory and common sense), and criterion-related or predictive validity (the degree to which these 12 conditions occur with the desired business outcomes). Empirical validity was tested via meta-analysis (i.e., based on the cumulative results of a number of other studies). This confirmed that these 12 conditions are, indeed, associated with the 4 business results — employee retention, customer retention, productivity, and profitability.

[21] Emery, M. (ed.) (1993). *Participative design for participative democracy*. Canberra, NSW: Australian National University.

[22] Adapted from: Hiebert, M., and Klatt, B. (2001). *The encyclopedia of leadership: A practical guide to popular leadership theories and techniques*. New York, NY: McGraw-Hill, p. 126–8.

[23] Covey, S.R. (1989). *The 7 habits of highly effective people: Powerful lessons in personal change*. New York, NY: Simon & Schuster.

[24] Walton, Richard E. (1985) "From Control to Commitment in the Workplace," *Harvard Business Review*, (March-April) p. 77–84.

[25] Ibid, p. 77.

[26] The distinction between *teams* and *workgroups* is fully examined in: Katzenbach, J.R., and Smith, D.K., (1993). *The wisdom of teams: Creating the high-performance organization*. New York, NY: HarperBusiness.

[27] Boehm, B.W. (1981). *Software economics*. Englewood Cliffs, NJ: Prentice-Hall, p. 39–40.

[28] Graham, A.K. (2000). "Beyond Performance Management 101: Lessons for Managing Large Development Programs," *Project Management Journal*, (December) p. 9.

[29] Treasury Board of Canada Secretariat. *Modernizing accountability practices in the public sector*. <http://www.tbs-sct.gc.ca/rma/account/oagtbs_e.asp>

[30] Report to the honorable Dan Burton, Chairman, Committee on Government Reform, House of Representatives (October, 2000). *Managing for results: Emerging benefits from selected agencies' use of performance agreements*. GAO–01-115.

[31] Treasury Board of Canada Secretariat. *Modernizing accountability practices in the public sector*. <http://www.tbs-sct.gc.ca/rma/account/oagtbs_e.asp>

[32] Ibid.

[33] Ibid.

[34] Ibid.

[35] Report to the honorable Dan Burton, Chairman, Committee on Government Reform, House of Representatives (October, 2000). *Managing for results: Emerging benefits from selected agencies' use of performance agreements*. GAO–01-115.

[36] Ibid.

[37] Ibid.

[38] This scandal in 1999 at the Canadian government ministry, Human Resources Development Canada (HRDC) became known as the 'billion dollar boondoggle' when poor accounting practices at HRDC left close to a billion dollars of job-creation funds unaccounted for.

[39] Angier, M. (March 3, 2003). *Your agreements show your integrity*. Success Networks International <www.positivepath.net/ideasMA29.asp>.

[40] Carver, John. (1991) *Boards that make a difference: A new design for leadership in nonprofit and public organizations*. San Francisco, CA: Jossey-Bass.

Index

A

About Murphy Klatt Consulting

Bruce Klatt, MA and Shaun Murphy, PhD lead an organization of consultants specializing in four areas:

- **Accountability/Alignment**™: Focuses individual and team energy to achieve corporate strategy.
- **Project Services**: We support project organizations from the early planning stages through to design and implementation. Services include guidance on project agreements, organization design, and resourcing; building performance oriented leadership teams and project work cultures; and independent project reviews/audits, contract planning, risk analysis and mitigation.
- **Organizational Effectiveness**: We contribute to the effectiveness of executive and management teams, and assist organizations to implement corporate strategy using change management tools.
- **Leadership Coaching**: We have a wealth of experience coaching high performing executives.

Murphy Klatt Consulting Inc.
Calgary – Halifax – Victoria
Suite 630 – 1207, 11th Avenue SW
Calgary, Alberta, Canada T3C 0M5

phone: (403) 278 • 3821
toll free: 1 (877) 878 • 3821
fax: (403) 278 • 1403
e-mail: mail@murphyklatt.com
websites: www: murphyklatt.com

Accountability/Alignment Online

NOW YOU CAN ALIGN, ONLINE!

Visit <**www.accountabilityalignment.com**> to view a demonstration of our on-line facilitation process, and to access the resources that will enable you to write your own Accountability Agreement®, and align with others in your organization. The site also provides various examples of Accountability Agreements® and alignment resources.

Benefits Include:

- An electronically facilitated process through which you will be guided and challenged as you develop your Accountability Agreement.
- An online process to facilitate alignment across your entire team.
- The ability to access and update your Accountability Agreement from anywhere in the world.
- The ability to view the Accountability Agreement of anyone in your organization, or use the search function to find individuals accountable for specific functions or projects.
- Online consulting support. If you need help completing or aligning your Accountability Agreement our consultants are available online, by phone, or in person.
- It's safe, secure, and easy to use.